*Education Interest Groups
in the Nation's Capital*

Education Interest Groups

in the Nation's Capital.

STEPHEN K. BAILEY
Vice-President ''
American Council on Education

AMERICAN COUNCIL ON EDUCATION   •   *Washington, D.C.*

Library of Congress Cataloging in Publication Data
Bailey, Stephen Kemp.
    Education interest groups in the Nation's Capital.
    Includes index.
    1. Education and state—United States. 2. Pres-
sure groups. 3. Lobbying. I. Title.
LC89.B33   379.73   75-22279
ISBN 0-8268-1265-1

To
John F. Morse
In appreciation and with profound respect

Contents

Preface

THIS MONOGRAPH treats of education interest groups in the nation's capital. It attempts to describe who they are, whom they represent, what they want, how they function, and something of the tasks they face in the proximate future. The time is the mid-1970s, with occasional dips into the near past.

The reasons for undertaking such a work are easily summarized. First, nothing quite like it exists, and educators and politicians, and the students of both, do not reason well or plan well in a state of ignorance. Second, at this writing, education in the United States suffers from an ebb tide of public support, and its friends need to consider whatever instruments or agencies exist to help it escape a dangerous fiscal and programmatic undertow. And, third, historic shifts are occurring in federal intra- and inter-branch relations as well as in federal-state-local relations; these shifts place new demands on education's representatives, some of whom may profit from a fresh, if brief, presentation of present realities and of the troubled currents ahead.

A comment is due each of these items.

Although a number of articles and books describe aspects of the world of educational policy making in Washington, no comprehensive summary of Washington-based organizations and associations at all educational levels exists. The lack is remarkable. Education interest groups have been in existence for many decades, but in the 1950s and 1960s the dramatic increase in federal contracts, grants, and formula aid served as a magnet to draw distant association headquarters like iron filings to the field of force of the nation's capital. Inasmuch as few scholars or pamphleteers have deemed the migration suitable for extended description and analysis, one can only conclude that some combination of practitioner reticence and scholarly preoccupation has conspired to keep matters unilluminated.

The first serious article on the politics of American education was written by Thomas H. Eliot in 1959, and a few years later this writer coauthored the first book on the subject.[1] Since then, several younger scholars have entered the field, but the pickings are still slim. As I had reason to note in the preface of *Schoolmen and Politics*, "Academics with an interest in the sociology of knowledge could well address themselves to the question why it is that the two areas in our political culture that take the biggest slices of public money, defense at the national level and education at the state and local levels, have received so little attention from professional political scientists."[2]

In this connection, it is useful to remember that during the 1960s education associations in Washington found themselves on an escalator of public approbation and intimate political support in high places. Johnson as President; Wayne Morse in the Senate; Adam Clayton Powell in the House; Anthony Celebrezze, John Gardner, and Wilbur Cohen in the Department of Health, Education, and Welfare; Frank Keppel and Harold Howe in the Office of Education; Ralph Huitt and Samuel Halperin in legislative liaison; Douglass Cater in the White House—who needed external educational influence? Viewed from the White House, from HEW, and from the Hill, education associations were frequently considered fractious contenders to be placated and homogenized, not centers of innovation and constructive energy. It is a fair reading of history to suggest that the legislative largesse of the mid-1960s was less a tribute to education's Washington representatives, granted a few heroic

1. Eliot, "Towards an Understanding of Public School Politics," *American Political Science Review*, December 1959, pp. 1032–51. Stephen K. Bailey et al., *Schoolmen and Politics: A Study of State Aid to Education in the Northeast* (Syracuse, N.Y.: Syracuse University Press, 1962).

2. *Schoolmen and Politics*, p. viii.

exceptions, than to President Johnson's sense of national priorities and to U.S. Commissioner of Education Francis Keppel's
negotiating skills.

How quickly a world can change! At the federal level, with
respect to support for education, retrenchment has succeeded
expansion; skepticism has replaced blind faith; Vietnam con-
quered Johnson's interest in high-level funding for education;
Presidents Nixon and Ford replaced Johnson; Morse and Powell
are dead; Celebrezze, Gardner, Cohen, Keppel, Howe, Huitt,
Cater, and Halperin are scattered to diverse private or judicial
undertakings. In the executive branch, educational policies have
been fashioned by an uncertain admixture of homespun rhetoric
and slide-rule rigor, and its educational structure has been broken
up and dispersed.

Inflation and recession, as this monograph is being written,
are having untoward effects on American education, ranging
from the serious to the catastrophic. But even if the general
economy could be quickly stabilized, there is no guarantee that
additional federal revenues would be earmarked for appropriations to education. Actually, most friends of education in the
federal bureaucracy are deeply worried.

On the legislative side, after a burst of energy in the Education Amendments of 1972, Congress has seemed almost unnerved, drained of energy by a decade of fecundity and by the
painful realization that many of its myriad legislative offspring
in the field of education were stillborn or are palpably retarded.
The renewal of authorizations in 1974 for the Elementary-Secondary Education Act of 1965 was a protracted and debilitating
—if steadfast—struggle on all sides.

Information for this study has come largely from interviews
and from brochures, flyers, pamphlets, newsletters, charters, and
congressional documents. James Browne of the Institute for
Educational Leadership of the George Washington University

gave generously of his time during six weeks in the winter of 1972–73 to assist in an arduous interviewing schedule. I am grateful for his expert interrogations and for his helpful insights. They inform most of the pages of this study. I am also indebted to the more than two hundred officials, members of Congress, legislative staff members, and education representatives who submitted to extensive questioning or who responded generously to written inquiries. Their understanding and interest has made this monograph possible. Special thanks must also be extended to Norman Drachler, Samuel Halperin, and Michael O'Keefe, 1972–73 colleagues in the Institute for Educational Leadership, who gave me support and advice on innumerable occasions and whose kind offer to become the Institute's first scholar-in-residence provided an ideal financial and physical base for my research. Samuel Halperin read the manuscript in penultimate form, as did George Arnstein, Lawrence Gladieux, Charles B. Saunders, Jr., Sheldon Elliot Steinbach, and Stanley McFarland. All have saved me embarrassment by discovering errors and by suggesting new facts or interpretations. Finally, the constant and efficient assistance of my wife, Cornelia W. Bailey, and my former secretary, Rosemary Halko, and my present secretary, Marcia Collette, can never be adequately acknowledged.

One additional comment must be made. I did not know when I undertook the study that I was to become, as of May 1, 1973, the vice-president of the American Council on Education. That decision was made late in January 1973, in the middle of my peripatetic research. What effect this decision has had on my perception of others or their perception of me is impossible to gauge. It made me more conscious of the dedicated work carried on over several years, with inadequate assistance, by individual government relations officers in a number of associations. All of us charged with association responsibilities stand on their shoulders. I have tried not to trim or temper my interpretations of reality as a result of my new assignment. I have been around too long, however, to contend that personal fortunes can be kept totally separate from scholarly attitudes. The reader, thus warned, may apply variable discounts as he comes across words or phrases that seem self-serving or biased.

In any case, as sole author, I am fully aware that responsibility for the substance and style are mine. It goes without saying that what follows is a personal statement and not in any way an ACE position paper. Finally, the various associations mentioned in the text are meant to serve as examples. The omission of any given organization should not be construed as indicating a judgment about its value or importance.

STEPHEN K. BAILEY

CHAPTER ONE

The National Need for Education Spokesmen

THE FUTURE of American education at all levels is and will in no small measure be shaped by political decision-makers. Correlatively, only those who understand appropriate political influence can be effective in furthering educational policy goals.

Although certain education leaders and reformers have been well known for their political virtuosity, most education practitioners have, for generations, gone to extraordinary lengths to protect education's reputation for political innocence. Reticence about its special-interest and political activities is understandable. An attentive American public has wanted somehow to ensure that education was not subjected to national political domination on the one hand or to courthouse patronage on the other. To this end, it supported those leaders who fashioned special arrangements for semiautonomous educational governance at the state and local levels and in the private sector and those who, in the spirit of Article X of the U.S. Constitution, fostered the myth that education was not the federal government's business. These public sensibilities were reinforced by the concern of college administrators and faculties for institutional independence and of public school teachers and supervisors for occupational dignity and professional status. In consequence, the myth was further cultivated that politics and education do not mix, a myth supported by those town and city fathers and mothers who, for high motives, wanted politics kept out of the classroom and who, perhaps for more complex motives, wanted teachers kept out of politics.

At the national level, representatives of education organizations and associations, no matter how they behaved in fact, tended to adopt the protective rhetoric of political innocence cultivated back home. Their immunities under the First Amendment were rarely acknowledged. Instead they rationalized their way through the murk of lobby laws, attempting to walk a tight rope between prohibited "lobbying" and representational ineffectiveness. It is a dismaying reality of American politics that lobby laws so written as to amuse big oil industries or big defense contractors have unnerved scores of education's petitioners who fear that if they exercise their constitutional rights, they will violate Section 501(c)(3) of the Internal Revenue Code and thereby lose their tax-exempt status.

For whatever reasons, most education representatives in Washington have not sought publicity for their activities, even though reports to their constituencies are laden with descriptions of accomplishment.

Now, to those who believe in the importance of education to the national interest and in education's need for continuing and increasing federal support, it is clear that education's spokesmen in the nation's capital have a new and important role to play—a role of unprecedented creativity and leadership.

The education community basked for decades in the sun of self-evident virtue. Education associations rarely had to explain education's raison d'être, and they often seemed embarrassed by and defensive about the federal government's interest in them. As late as 1952, the Commission on Financing Higher Education of the Association of American Universities had issued a unanimous report calling for "a halt . . . to the introduction of new programs of direct federal aid to colleges and university . . . [or to expanding] the scope of its scholarship aid to individual students."[1] The idea of substantial federal aid to precollegiate education was so unsettling to the parties concerned that year after year they let authorizing bills founder on the triple shoals of "federal control," "race," and "religion."

In the mid-1970s, American education feels substantially embattled. The reasons need only be sketched: the campus disruptions and disaffections of the 1960s; the skyrocketing costs of all education, exacerbated by general inflation and by the energy crisis; the leveling-off of the birthrate; the patent inefficacies of schooling for many of the nation's minorities and the uncertain effects of compensatory policies; teacher militancy and strikes; the sullen impact of the busing issue; the alleged drug on the labor market of certain categories of college graduates and higher-degree holders; a sense that education's leaders have lost their way. These and other factors have conspired to lead to a popular disenchantment with education as an elixir for all personal and social pain. A taxpayer's revolt has manifested itself, directly, in local votes on bond issues and education budgets and, indirectly, in the behavior of elected executives and legislators both in the states and in the nation's capital.

The time has come when education's representatives must defend the need for assigning to education a far higher priority than it now receives on the national government's policy agenda. They must strive for a restructuring of educational agencies in the Department of Health, Education, and Welfare and in the executive branch generally. They must search for financial support and for regulatory policies that do not have stifling effects on institutions and localities. They must find avenues of access to new levels and temperaments of decision-makers in both the legislative and executive branches. They must become far more sophisticated than heretofore in the electoral aspects of congres-

1. Laura C. Ford, "Institutional Aid," *Journal of Law and Education,* October 1972, p. 541.

sional and Presidential politics. They must extend their concerns to state and local education decision-makers, who are becoming increasingly powerful. They must cultivate other powerful interest groups in the society. And in making their case to legislative and executive sponsors, they must discover ways to do so that anticipate or respond promptly to the immediate operational needs of those sponsors and their staffs.

The assignment becomes herculean in that education's representatives in Washington must do all of this at a time when inflation and economic uncertainty are rampant and power relationships between the executive and legislative branches are particularly complex. The economic and political uncertainties are further complicated by changes in membership on key committees and by new budget procedures within the Congress—factors that can muddle education's recently earned knowledge about how to relate effectively to congressional appropriations committees.

Education groups tended understandably to side with the Congress in the "impounding" and "New Federalism" fights with the executive branch during the Nixon administration. Court decisions and the accession of President Ford have changed this picture. As yet, however, few education associations have diversified their portfolios of influence to include the studied cultivation of executive branch policy offices and officials. Even fewer associations pay adequate attention to the state of the political art exercised by their regional and local affiliates and clienteles in state capitals and in major local governments. This last can become increasingly troublesome.

Revenue flows that appear and disappear before the eyes of education's petitioners in Washington continue to emerge in various shapes and sizes at the state and local levels. If these monies are not to be dissipated as tax relief bonanzas or as sops to state highway lobbies, education interests—particularly higher education interests—must increase by several cubits their capacity to influence the allocations at state and local levels. Insofar as Washington-based education representatives can help their state and local affiliates and their grass-roots clientele to understand these developments and these necessities, they will have performed a vital service.

The focus of this monograph, however, is Washington. As far ahead as anyone can see, the federal government will exercise a crucial leverage on the future of American education. Federal laws and regulations in such fields as tax policy, collective bargaining, student aid, equal rights, research, energy policy, antirecession policies, and a host of other issues, directly or indirectly affecting education, do have and can have an enormous impact on the future of the entire educational enterprise. The national need for effective spokesmen for education was never greater. This belief prompted the research and drafting reflected in the following pages.

CHAPTER TWO

Interest Groups and Whom They Represent

DEPENDENT upon definition, there are somewhere between two hundred and fifty and three hundred education associations, organizations, and institutional representatives located in or near the nation's capital. All told, these associations, organizations, and agents purport to speak for more than 70 million people who are engaged or deeply involved in the American educational enterprise—one third of the nation's population.

To understand the bewildering variety of education interests represented in the Washington area, one must begin by recognizing the pervasive pluralism of their constituency. For example, one major interest group in American education is certainly "teachers." But do we really mean *one* major interest group? There are public school teachers and private school teachers; nursery school teachers and high school teachers; junior college faculty and graduate school faculty; French teachers and mathematics teachers; medical school faculty and engineering school faculty; paraprofessional teachers and licensed teachers; teacher aides and guidance counselors; black teachers and white teachers; men teachers and women teachers; tenured teachers and non-tenured teachers; vocational education teachers and football coaches; teachers of the handicapped and teachers of the gifted; AFT-affiliated teachers, NEA-affiliated teachers, and AAUP-affiliated teachers.

Not all of these segments are housed in separate organiza-

6

tions replete with Washington representatives, but many of
them are.

And "teachers" is only one category of educators. There are
supervisors and principals, superintendents and school board
members, business officers and public relations specialists, college presidents and boards of trustees, deans and provosts,
maintenance employees and research directors. There are the
diverse consumers of education: parents, pupils, students, adults.
There are profit and nonprofit organizations whose viability
depends on satisfying the educational markets: the testing in-
dustry, book publishers, creators of audio-visual hardware and
software, school bus dealers, school architects, chalk manufacturers, locker salesmen, purveyors of laboratory chemicals, and
shippers of experimental mice. There is education's major logis-
tical adjunct: the diverse system of school, public, and research
libraries.

There are combinations of interests by level of education: preschool, K–12, postsecondary proprietary, two-year college, four-
year college and university, adult and continuing education.
There are regional groupings of educational institutions like the
Western Interstate Commission for Higher Education. There are
those interested in the relevance of education to specific social
issues: for example, poverty, civil rights. There are religious
interests that cut across all levels of education; there are also
religious interests divided according to level of education. There
are research interests of all kinds, including research about education itself. There are those interested in the education of
veterans, of blacks, of Indians, of Mexican-Americans, of the
aged. There are education agents or agencies sponsored by individual states, collections of states, or groups of institutions.
Not all of these definable interests have formal associations,
Washington offices, and assigned representatives; but most do.

Where does one end?

And what does one do about noneducational interests? One

answer would be to ignore them. But how, then, does one categorize the AFL/CIO legislative staff (as distinct from the staff of the American Federation of Teachers), which is widely believed to be one of the most powerful educational forces in Washington; or the National Farmers Union which, during the original House fight for the Elementary-Secondary Education Act of 1965, mustered more volunteer citizen lobbyists (250 farm people) on Capitol Hill than any other national organization; or the National League of Cities and the United States Conference of Mayors, both of which have educational components?

The truth is that the taxonomic problem, with its combinations and permutations, defies tidy categorization. In a short monograph, the best one can do is select a fairly arbitrary classification system and then list a few associations that illustrate each type. In describing in short compass any complex universe or multiverse, categories are bound to overlap, and the edges of each category must remain fuzzy. The ten categories selected will, it is hoped, help the uninitiate perceive some of the major outlines. To the sophisticate, each category may well raise further descriptive and taxonomic issues. For a categorical overview, see Figure 1.

I. Umbrella Organizations

The first category includes broad-based organizations that have highly diverse institutional and associational memberships and, perhaps, affiliates. A few years ago, the National Education Association of the United States would have qualified as the prototype of umbrella organizations but it has now become predominantly a teachers union.

Two major examples of Washington-based umbrella organizations in education are the American Council on Education and the Committee for Full Funding of Education Programs.

The American Council on Education does not have persons as

WASHINGTON-BASED EDUCATION REPRESENTATION: TYPOLOGY AND EXAMPLES

I. **Umbrella organizations**
American Council on Education
Committee for Full Funding of Education Programs

II. **Institutional associations**
American Association of Community and Junior Colleges
Association of Independent Colleges and Schools

III. **Teachers unions**
National Education Association of the United States
American Federation of Teachers
American Association of University Professors

IV. **Professions, fields, and disciplines**
Music Educators National Conference
American Political Science Association
Association of American Medical Colleges

V. **Librarians, suppliers, and technologists**
American Library Association
National Audio-Visual Association, Inc.
College Entrance Examination Board

VI. **Religion, race, sex**
National Catholic Educational Association
Washington Research Project Action Council
American Association of University Women

VII. **"Lib-lab" (liberal, labor) lobbies**
AFL/CIO
National Farmers Union

VIII. **Institutions and institutional systems**
Pennsylvania State University
New York State Education Department

IX. **Administrators and boards**
American Association of School Administrators
National School Boards Association
Association of Governing Boards of Universities
and Colleges
Council of Chief State School Officers

X. **Miscellaneous**
Council for Basic Education
National Committee for Citizens in Education
National Student Lobby

FIG. 1

members. It is a conglomerate of institutions and associations. It has three classes of membership: Constituent Organization Members, Associated Organization Members, and Institutional Members. It also has Affiliates. The first category is divided into Groups A and B.

Group A comprises an inner group of major higher education associations or interests: American Association of Community and Junior Colleges; American Association of State Colleges and Universities; Association of American Colleges; Association of American Universities; Association of Jesuit Colleges and Universities; Association of Urban Universities; National Association of State Universities and Land-Grant Colleges; and the National Catholic Educational Association. Group B includes more than 60 associations, councils, and commissions that represent specific functional or professional interests. The Group B list includes, for example: American Association of Colleges for Teacher Education, American Association of Dental Schools, American Association of University Professors, American Library Association, American Political Science Association, Association of American Medical Colleges, College Entrance Examination Board, National Association of College and University Business Officers, Phi Delta Kappa, and Speech Communication Association.

Associated organization members include 114 regional and national institutes, centers, boards, associations, and societies that range across a wide spectrum of educational interests. For example, among the associated organization members are: American Federation of Teachers, NEA, Smithsonian Institution, United Negro College Fund, Inc., New York State Education Department, Brookings Institution, Teachers Insurance and Annuity Association, and Institute of European Studies.

ACE has almost 1,400 institutional members including nearly all of the universities, most of the four-year colleges, and about one-third of the accredited community and junior colleges in the nation.

Finally, there are two groups of affiliates totaling 57 members: Group A is made up of institutions, libraries, and secondary schools; Group B, of nonprofit educational organizations, foundations, fraternities, and societies. Under the former may be found the New York Public Library and the School for International Training, in Brattleboro, Vermont. In the latter are included the American Bankers Association—Education Group, Boy Scouts of America, Salk Institute for Biological Studies, and Sears-Roebuck Foundation.

Such a vast and diverse constituency hides the reality that in the deliberations of ACE some members have traditionally had a greater voice than others. It is scarcely coincidence that, of the past thirteen chairmen, the Ivy League and the prestigious land-grant universities have provided more than half, and that all ACE chairmen have been college or university presidents. This traditional pattern is now shifting. In addition, conscious efforts have recently been made to enlarge and increase the representativeness of ACE's commissions, committees, and board, although college and university executives continue to exercise preponderant influence in ACE activities.

The Committee for Full Funding of Education Programs (until 1972 known as the "Emergency Committee . . .") was created in 1969 through the good offices of NEA, AFL/CIO, National School Boards Association, and a catalyst from the Detroit school system. Technically, it is not a formal association or lobby. It is a loose conglomerate of education interest groups bound together by a common concern for the level of federal appropriations for education. The committee was a response to the growing gap between what was authorized by congressional action for various educational programs and what was actually appropriated. Vietnam expenditures first created the gap during President Johnson's administration, and the gap widened during the first Nixon administration. Although the committee has claimed up to 250 contributors, its associational and institutional membership has fluctuated from roughly fifty to eighty, and only a handful of organizations have represented the inner core of the activity. The fact that this core has involved both K–12 and postsecondary associations, however, has made the committee the most comprehensive education organization, in power-political terms, in the Washington area. It was housed for most of its life in the Congressional Hotel, across the street from House Office Buildings, and is now located at 148 Duddington Place, S.E. The work of the committee has been directed from the beginning by the capable legislative strategist Charles W. Lee, formerly professional staff member of the Senate Subcommittee on Education.

II. Institutional Associations

The second category is largely confined to the realm of post-secondary education and includes associations of a particular class or type of institution. A precollegiate example is the recently formed Council for American Private Education, in Washington, which represents private elementary and secondary education. The major exemplars of category II are the American Association of Community and Junior Colleges, the American Association of State Colleges and Universities, the Association of American Colleges, the Association of American Universities, the National Association of State Universities and Land-Grant Colleges, and the Association of Independent Colleges and Schools. Essentially, each of these is a collection of educational institutions that share some attribute of size, status, location, historical background, or underlying purpose.

To the uninitiated, the nomenclature is confusing. Why, for example, should there be an American Association of State Colleges and Universities and also the National Association of State Universities and Land-Grant Colleges? And why a separate Association of American Universities? A separate Association of American Colleges?

The answer is less logical than historical. Each of the institutional associations emerged as the expression of a peculiar confluence of circumstances. Although there is patent overlap in membership and function among many of the institutional associations, each has its own focus of concern and interest. And, as noted later, there is more communication, sharing, and rationalization of common workloads than a superficial listing of organizations suggests. Figure 2 gives a brief introduction to representative institutional associations.

To this list might be added the National Council of Independent Colleges and Universities, although it is so umbilically related to the Association of American Colleges, which staffs it, as to make separate mention a bit redundant. In essence, NCICU is the private sector of AAC plus additional non-AAC private institutions. Its total membership is larger by 300 than that of its parent association.

Most of the institutional associations are headquartered in the National Center for Higher Education at One Dupont Circle—the exceptions being AAC and NCICU. Cooperating on most large issues, going their separate ways on others, the institutional associations are occasionally plagued by various kinds of identity crises and fiscal uncertainties. Yet singly and together they constitute an important aspect of education's representation in Washington.

III. *Teachers Unions*

K–12 teachers, in the generic sense, are represented in Washington by the National Education Association and by the American Federation of Teachers. At the postsecondary level, the American Association of University Professors has been, and is, the predominant voice of college faculty members, although both the AFT and the NEA have developed aggressive college-level membership drives.

NEA has a dues-paying membership of more than 1.5 million

INSTITUTIONAL ASSOCIATIONS

Name	Founded	Number of Institutions, 1974-75	Orientation or Nature
American Association of Community and Junior Colleges	1920	905	Public and private two-year colleges and technical institutes
American Association of State Colleges and Universities	1961	315	Regional state colleges and universities (as distinct from major state university centers), representing 25 percent of the student population in four-year colleges
Association of American Colleges	1915	780	Public and private four-year colleges of liberal arts and sciences
Association of American Universities	1948	48	Forty-six prestigious research-oriented universities, public and private, in the United States; two Canadian universities
Association of Independent Colleges and Schools	1972	482	(Formerly United Business Schools Association) Proprietary business schools and colleges
Council for the Advancement of Small Colleges	1956	140	Small (under 2,000 students) private four-year colleges of liberal arts and sciences
National Association of State Universities and Land-Grant Colleges	1887	130	The principal public universities of the 50 states; 71 land-grant colleges and universities

FIG. 2

teachers, making it by far the largest professional organization in the world. In addition NEA has a number of affiliated organizations and departments that either share the facilities of 1201 Sixteenth Street, N.W., Washington, or derive services or prestige from some form of NEA connection. There are also a few nonaffiliated organizations that occupy space in 1201 Sixteeth Street and enjoy the benefits of propinquity to NEA and its affiliates. (See Figure 3.)

In the past few years, NEA has changed its traditional character dramatically. For decades the major umbrella for all the diverse groups associated with American public schools (and long dominated by administrators and supervisors), NEA in the early 1970s became for all intents and purposes a teachers union. Its administrative and supervisory components disaffiliated and moved to nearby Virginia. NEA's governmental relations office, under the able direction of Stanley J. McFarland, has a staff of twenty-four, including eight field representatives, six Washington lobbyists, and three political tacticians. Through the Coalition of American Public Employees (CAPE)—a political action organization which includes NEA, Treasury Department employees, and the American Federation of State, County and Municipal Employees—the National Education Association has become deeply involved in the campaign and electoral processes of the nation. In collective bargaining, it is in competition with the American Federation of Teachers and, at the higher education level, with the American Association of University Professors as well.

The American Federation of Teachers has a membership of 450,000: 410,000 K–12 teachers and 40,000 college faculty members. Its strength is largely in the urban centers of predominantly urban states. Until recently, the Washington office of AFT was not viewed by most observers as a center of policy power. With the election of Albert Shanker, of New York, as national president, however, changes toward aggressive action are virtually

NATIONAL EDUCATION ASSOCIATION
DEPARTMENTS, NATIONAL AFFILIATES,
AND ASSOCIATED ORGANIZATIONS

(January 1, 1975)

Departments
American Driver and Traffic Safety Education Association
Rural Education Association
Department of School Nurses

National Affiliates
National Art Education Association
Association for Educational Communications and Technology
National Association of Educational Secretaries
American Association of Elementary-Kindergarten-Nursery
   Educators
American Alliance for Health, Physical Education, and
   Recreation
Home Economics Education Association
American Industrial Arts Association
Journalism Education Association
National Council of Teachers of Mathematics
Music Educators National Conference
National Association for Public Continuing and Adult
   Education
National Retired Teachers Association
National Association of School Counselors
National Council for the Social Studies

Associated Organizations
National Business Education Association
Association for Educational Data Systems
Council for Exceptional Children
NTL Institute for Applied Behavioral Science
American Association of School Librarians
National School Public Relations Association
Speech Communication Association
National Science Teachers Association

FIG. 3

inevitable. Shanker has pledged a well-funded campaign to organize college faculties; he is politically oriented and politically sophisticated; he is a powerful presence in the councils of the AFL/CIO, thereby creating high drama in his challenge to NEA's unofficial link to the centers of power within organized labor, through Jerry Wurf, president of the American Federation of State, County and Municipal Employees.

IV. Professions, Fields, and Disciplines

More than 30 Washington-based education organizations are structured around a professional field or an academic discipline; in addition, a number of other subject-matter associations are headquartered in other parts of the country. Again, a rough division must be made between secondary and postsecondary associations (see Figure 4), although a few organizations like Music Educators National Conference involve educators from all levels—preschool through university. A further subdivision appears at the higher education levels where some subject-matter associations include both undergraduate and graduate interests, whereas others—particularly in the professions—are graduate level only. Figure 4 lists some of the major subject-matter associations that have headquarters in the Washington area.

Although most of the subject-matter associations are affiliated with either NEA or ACE, and have overlapping memberships with one or more other associations, their major focus tends to be limited to the well-being of a particular professional field or academic discipline.

V. Librarians, Suppliers, and Technologists

Among the major influential associations which are active in Washington and have special interests in education are those concerned with books and with educational materials and technology. It is quite impossible to list all of the industries and interest groups in the nation's capital that have such concerns.

TYPICAL SUBJECT-MATTER ASSOCIATIONS
IN THE WASHINGTON AREA

Precollegiate
American Alliance for Health, Physical Education, and
  Recreation
American Association of Physics Teachers
American Driver and Traffic Safety Education Association
American Industrial Arts Association
American Vocational Association
National Association of Biology Teachers, Inc.
National Council for the Social Studies
National Council of Teachers of Mathematics
National Science Teachers Association

Postsecondary
American Association for the Advancement of Science
American Association of Colleges for Teacher Education
American Association of Colleges of Pharmacy
American Educational Research Association
American Historical Association
American Political Science Association
American Psychological Association
American Society for Engineering Education
Association of American Law Schools
Association of American Medical Colleges
Association of Schools of Allied Health Professions
Mathematical Association of America
National Association of Schools of Music

FIG. 4

Among the most important are the American Library Association, Association of Research Libraries, National Audio-Visual Association, Inc., Association of American Publishers, Inc., Association for Educational Communications and Technology, the Joint Council on Educational Telecommunications, the National Association of Educational Broadcasters, and the Council on Instruction and Professional Development of the NEA.

The American Library Association is the major spokesman for the universe of public libraries. Founded in 1876, it represents more than 37,000 libraries, librarians, publishing houses, business firms, and individuals. Its power on the Washington scene stems from its able leadership and the size, geographic spread, and local prestige of its constituents.

The Association of Research Libraries was founded in 1931. Today it represents the interests of the ninety-odd major research libraries in the United States and Canada. It includes large university libraries, the three national libraries of the United States (the Library of Congress, the National Agricultural Library, and the National Library of Medicine), and a number of special libraries with substantial research collections such as the New York Public Library and the Center for Research Libraries in Chicago.

The National Audio-Visual Association consists chiefly of private enterprise manufacturers and dealers who sell everything from simple viewers to complex audio-visual equipment. Their markets include educators and trainers in all fields of endeavor. A few book publishers are members, but dealers predominate on the board of directors.

As its name implies, the Association of American Publishers represents the nation's major book publishers—about 275 firms. It tends to be dominated by the large houses that have substantial interests in text and reference works.

The Association for Educational Communications and Technology, founded in 1923, is a professional organization whose members are active in the systematic planning, application, and production of communication media for instruction. Representing a wide spectrum of responsibilities in education, AECT's 21,000 members and subscribers can be found in schools, universities, government agencies, museums, and wherever significant pedagogic change is under way.

The Joint Council on Educational Telecommunications is a consortium of more than twenty of the nation's leading non-profit organizations in education and communications, including ACE and NEA and many of their organizational associates. Established in 1950 to provide leadership in persuading the Federal Communications Commission to reserve TV channels for noncommercial broadcasting, JCET serves as education's established instrument for coordination and participation in the arena of communications policy making.

The National Association of Educational Broadcasters is nearly fifty years old. It represents a variety of related interests: for example, educational TV stations, educational radio (mostly FM) stations, and radio and TV training institutions. NAEB and JCET are the major spokesmen in Washington for education's interests in telecommunications.

The College Entrance Examination Board, a broad-based association with membership spanning both postsecondary and secondary education, is responsible for the major college admissions testing program in the country as well as the most heavily utilized needs analysis system in the field of student financial aid. Its Washington presence has been important in related areas of federal policy. The Educational Testing Service, the organization in Princeton, New Jersey, which administers CEEB examinations and engages in a variety of other activities and programs on contract, also maintains a Washington office, as does the Iowa City–based American College Testing Program, the principal competitor of CEEB-ETS in the admissions testing field.

The Council on Instruction and Professional Development of

NEA was formed in 1972 by a merger of four NEA units: National Commission on Teacher Education and Professional Standards, Center for the Study of Instruction, Educational Technology Division, and Adult Education Service Division.

VI. Religion, Race, and Sex

The world of education has been shaken in the past several years by swirling controversies involving religion, race, poverty, and sex. The religious issue has centered largely on the question of government financial assistance to church-related schools and colleges. Here the great antagonists have been, on the one hand, the National Catholic Educational Association, the Department of Education of the United States Catholic Conference, the Association of Jesuit Colleges and Universities, and related Catholic associations (abetted on occasion by a few orthodox sects from Judaism and from Protestantism); on the other hand are Americans United for Separation of Church and State, the National Council of the Churches of Christ in the U.S.A., the American Civil Liberties Union, NEA, and AFT. Recent court decisions have so narrowed the range of policy possibilities for aiding sectarian education as to mute the intensity of church-state squabbles. Nevertheless, NCEA as the Catholic counterpart to NEA, the U.S. Catholic Conference (known as the "Bishops Conference"), and the Association of Jesuit Colleges and Universities remain powerful education advocates in the nation's capital.

Most of the important national civil rights organizations have had education as a major concern for more than twenty years. Internal dissensions and the Nixon years of "benign neglect," however, have slowed and dissipated the energies of those associations concentrating on the educational welfare of minorities. The Washington Research Project Action Council, the Leadership Conference on Civil Rights, the United Auto Workers, and a project at Catholic University (under William Taylor) have been major catalysts of cooperation. The National Association for the Advancement of Colored People and its affiliated Legal Defense and Educational Fund, Inc., continue to slog away at key issues that are deemed judicable. The Washington Research Project's interest extends beyond education to general concern with the welfare of children, especially children of the poor. The educational interests of Spanish-speaking Americans, both Puerto Ricans and Mexican-Americans, are represented by the National Congress of Hispanic American Citizens.

At the higher education level, the National Association for Equal Opportunity in Higher Education is the major voice of the nation's black colleges, although its interests extend to the far larger universe of minority opportunities throughout the postsecondary system.

Blatant inequalities in the treatment of women in education (all the way from admission policies and fellowship awards to tenured posts on faculty rosters and administrative posts in precollegiate education) have existed for generations. In recent years women have suddenly made a number of educational institutions and government policy-makers uncomfortably aware of these inequalities. The National Organization for Women (NOW) and Women's Equity Action League (WEAL) have been joined by three Washington-based organizations that have been increasingly aggressive in pressing for women's rights in education: Federation of Organizations for Professional Women, Interstate Association of Commissions on the Status of Women, and the American Association of University Women. Actually, an increasing number of education associations are enlarging their attention to the status of women. Indicative are Bernice Sandler's Project on the Status and Education of Women (of the Association of American Colleges), Resource Center on Sex Roles in Education (NEA), and the recent appointment by the American Council on Education of a full-time staff director,

Emily Taylor, whose sole concern is with "Women in Higher Education."

VII. *"Lib-Lab" Lobby*

Some years ago in discussing the coalitions that backed the passage of the Employment Act of 1946, I referred to a "lib-lab" lobby—a loose association of liberal and labor organizations that shared common social values. The lib-lab lobby for education is a different kind of organism from that which functioned under the Full Employment bill of 1945 (although the overlaps are notable). But the phrase (borrowed from British political history of a century ago) is useful in the latter-day context. Apart from a few hardy reform battalions like the United Auto Workers and the National Farmers Union that frequently work on educational issues, the lib-lab lobby for education can be virtually encompassed by reference to one central staff: the Legislative Department of the AFL/CIO.

The AFL/CIO is the largest organization of trade unions in the United States. It is composed of 110 national and international unions and enjoys a total dues-paying membership of over 14 million. Although the preponderance of power in the internal affairs of the AFL/CIO remains, as it has for years, in the hands of the skilled trades, the Washington-based Department of Legislation under the direction of former Congressman Andrew J. Biemiller tends, in a rather anomalous way, to represent an extension of the philosophy of such reformist giants of the industrial unionism of the 1930s as Sidney Hillman, Philip Murray, Walter Reuther, and David Dubinsky. The Gompers-Green tradition of the old American Federation of Labor (stick to bread-and-butter issues) seems light-years away from the legislative interests of Biemiller and his staff. It is true that their recent legislative reports start out with a heading called "Jobs and the Economy" and that "Labor Legislation" receives the second largest amount of attention. But other subtitles include "Housing and the Environment," "Health, Education, and Welfare," "Consumer Protection," "Civil Rights," "Civil Liberties," "Elections," "Congressional Reform," and "Foreign Affairs."

The interests of the AFL/CIO in education must be viewed as far broader than, and in many ways quite distinct from, the interests of its constituent American Federation of Teachers, although staff linkages between the two are increasingly organic. While the beginnings of the AFT go back to the 1930s, its present strength of members is largely a product of the struggles of the past decade. AFL/CIO's legislative interest in education, on the other hand, has deep historic roots. Kenneth Young, the highly professional assistant director of AFL/CIO's Department of Legislation, and for years in charge of its education portfolio, claims that labor's interest in education is as old as the movement itself. He points to a clause from the platform of the Ninth Convention of the AF of L in 1889: "the American Federation of Labor favors the greatest liberality by the United States and State Governments to further and advance the cause of the education of the masses." Labor, Young contends, has always seen in education an avenue to upward mobility and a key instrument in the equalization of bargaining strength. Whatever the historical background, the present reality in Washington is that the AFL/CIO is close to the center of the lib-lab coalition for federal support of education.

VIII. Institutions and Institutional Systems

On the roster of what is called the "Governmental Relations Group Luncheon," an ad hoc assemblage of Washington-based or Washington-oriented education representatives who eat together twice a month, there are listed roughly forty individual colleges, universities, state systems, or regional consortia. Some of these representatives are of considerable significance in the Washington scheme of things on matters educational. For example, no list of important education representatives would be complete without the names of Newton Cattell of Pennsylvania State University, P. Alistair MacKinnon of the State Education Department in Albany, Marilyn Berry representing the state of New Jersey, Ida Wallace representing a consortium of midwestern colleges, and Donald White and Peter Goldschmidt representing respectively the state of California and the University of California. Individually, these representatives have far more real influence than many of those associated with large Washington-based associations.

Some of them like MacKinnon cover all aspects of education at the state level. Some like Berry cover a variety of state interests, including but going beyond education. Others like Cattell are concerned with the interests of a single institution. But singly and together they are an important force in Washington education politics.

IX. *Administrators and Boards*

Top education administrators at the level of higher education tend to be represented through the institutional associations (Category II) noted earlier. But there is a variety of subordinate administrators who belong to Washington-based associations reflecting particular concerns: for example, the Council of Graduate Schools in the United States, the National University Extension Association, the National Association for Women Deans, Administrators, and Counselors, American College Health Association, Council for Advancement and Support of Education, National Association of College and University Attorneys, American Association of Collegiate Registrars and Admissions Officers, College and University Personnel Association, National Association of College and University Business Officers.

At the elementary and secondary levels, school administrators gravitate into one of four general associations or two functional associations. The four general associations are the Council of

Chief State School Officers, representing the fifty-five superintendents of instruction or commissioners of education in the several states and territories; the American Association of School Administrators, representing more than 12,000 local and district school superintendents; the National Association of Elementary School Principals, representing 24,000 principals of elementary schools; and the National Association of Secondary School Principals, representing approximately 27,000 junior high and high school principals. Neither of the last two has in its membership more than half of the total available number of principals respectively in the country.

Important Washington-based functional associations of school administrators include the National School Public Relations Association and the Association of School Business Officials of the United States and Canada. The former is housed across the Potomac in Arlington, Virginia, along with AASA, the National Academy for School Executives, the National Association of Educational Secretaries, and the National Association of Elementary School Principals. Both NSPRA and ASBO work closely with the major associations of school administrators noted above and with the National School Boards Association.

It is a long tradition in the United States to have educational institutions and systems under the policy direction of governing boards, at both lower and higher levels of education. For example, fifty-five of the fifty-seven states and territories have overarching boards of education (sometimes called boards of regents) which oversee categories of educational policy matters at the state level. Although the National Association of State Boards of Education (NASBE) is based in Denver, it maintains close contact with Washington policy directions through periodic meetings with key education associations that are Washington-based.

Without question, the most powerful organization representing members of governing boards is the National School Boards Association, representing 84,000 members of local school boards (sometimes called "school trustees"). Roughly 95 percent of all the nation's public school children fall under the responsibility of NSBA members. Technically, NSBA is a federation of state school board associations, but it has local school board affiliates and acts as more than an agent of state associations.

Although there is nothing in Washington comparable to NSBA at the higher education level, there is an Association of Governing Boards of Universities and Colleges, located at One Dupont Circle. AGB is an organization of members of boards of trustees of 500 institutions of higher education in the nation (roughly one-fifth of the total number of such institutions). In contrast to NSBA, AGB has traditionally viewed its functions in "non-governmental relations" terms, although this reticence is rapidly being overcome.

X. Miscellaneous

There is no adequate way of categorizing the sizable remainder of education interest groups in Washington. Some, like the National Student Lobby and the National Committee for Citizens in Education, are highly consumer-oriented; that is, they concern themselves with the welfare and rights of pupils and students and their parents. Others, like the Council for Basic Education, are concerned with the promotion and maintenance of quality at all levels of education. There is a range of Washington attorneys who represent, on a retainer basis, a variety of education clients on a number of issues but who rarely surface as "education representatives." Finally, but never finally, are the intermittent agents who come to town on behalf of one or a number of clients during a perceived crisis. The so-called Ad Hoc Group of some of America's most prestigious private research universities, had a tax expert monitoring the day-to-day ("minute-by-minute" would be more precise) tax reform deliberations of the House Ways and Means Committee during the summer and fall of 1974.

For purposes of analyzing the real influence structure in educational policy making in Washington, the categories noted above are, of course, almost totally useless. They suggest the range of interests, but neither their intensity nor their clout. Patently, some education interests are more powerful than others; some representatives are more astute and more energetic than others. Qualitative discriminations on such matters are always touchy and subjective, but some attempt has to be made if this monograph is to have any semblance of coherence and utility. Through interviews, and through a rough and impressionistic questionnaire sent to most of the key educational policymakers in the Education Division of HEW and on the staffs of congressional committees, the following Washington-based associations were rated at the top of the heap of "representational effectiveness" in the field of education policy: AFL/CIO, Committee for Full Funding of Education Programs, American Association of Community and Junior Colleges, American Vocational Association, Council for Exceptional Children, American Library Association, Association of Independent Colleges and Schools, National Education Association, NAACP, National Catholic Educational Association, Council of Chief State School Officers, the American Association of State Colleges and Universities, National Audio-Visual Association, American Council on Education, American Federation of Teachers, National Association of State Universities and Land-Grant Colleges, the National Student Lobby, and the National School Boards Association.

Any such list must, of course, be regarded with caution. It was compiled in 1973–74, and may not include some able newcomers. It misses a few extremely sophisticated education representatives who tend to work through others rather than directly. It misses the impact of certain specialists that are powerful in a limited field of interest: for example, the influence exerted by the College Entrance Examination Board on student aid legislation.

Nevertheless, the associations identified above were adjudged by a number of knowledgeable education specialists on Capitol Hill and in the executive branch of the federal government as important and influential. Most of these judgments have been confirmed by interviews with a range of education representatives themselves. The major argument would be over the size of the list. Among the heavily occupied insiders who work day-in and day-out on educational policy issues, any list of twenty is too long by two-thirds. For those not mentioned who know full well the impact their association has had upon particular facets of educational policy, twenty is obviously too fine a cut.

The only point to be made is that, of the 250–300 educational associations with Washington representation, only a relatively few are recognized as having substantial policy influence.

We have identified the various top associations earlier on, under various categories. But what in the way of generalizations can be made about the persons who represent these associations? They are, of course, a diverse lot. But certain common elements recur. Most were raised in America's hinterland, not in the Northeast. All have college degrees. Most have advanced degrees, either in law or education. Most have extensive professional experience in journalism, administration, or teaching. Virtually all of them have worked at some point in their careers on Capitol Hill, in the Department of Health, Education, and Welfare, or in other governmental or political settings.

What they want and how they operate are the subjects of the chapters that follow.

CHAPTER THREE

What They Want

IN A GENERIC SENSE, the question of what Washington-based education representatives want from the federal government can be answered quite simply: (1) protection for their clientele against harm, (2) rules and resources favorable to their clienteles' perceived interests, and (3) personal respectability and recognition. These, of course, are the basic wants of all those who attempt to influence the course of public policy, whatever the field of interest or level of government. The first two categories will be examined in this chapter, and the third, in chapter 5.

In the case of education, with its myriad facets and traditional localisms, a comprehensive delineation of specific wants is beyond possibility. The best that can be attempted is an impressionistic sample of discomfitures and needs that have surfaced in recent years in the nation's capital. The sample, it is hoped, may convey an accurate sense of a larger and infinitely more diverse reality.

Education interests, of course, often want contradictory things (more money, less control); they want different things (support for community colleges, support for research universities); or they want both collective action and autonomy in approaching influential authorities. The illustrations that follow evidence these and similar perversities.

Protection from Harm

The number of federal laws and administrative regulations that wittingly or unwittingly can do some kind of harm to various segments of American education is, in point of fact, staggering. Of these federal instruments, only a few directly concern formal educational policy. Fiscal policy, monetary policy, military policy, energy policy, wage-price policy, manpower policy, health policy, welfare policy, revenue-sharing policy, tax policy, copyright policy, telecommunications policy, civil rights and civil liberties policies, research policy, space policy—all of these, as well as the procedures for their implementation, can and do have profound effects on educational institutions and practices. Little wonder, then, that education representatives in the Washington area spend much of their time monitoring the day-to-day business of government in order to flag developments that might harm—and encourage developments that might help—one or more parts of the educational enterprise. Details of this monitoring activity are spelled out in chapter 4. Suffice it here to note that elaborate associational "radar screens" probe Congress, the courts, the executive agencies, the press, and other interest groups in a never-ending search for "significant" governmental actions.

Several disparate items suggest the reality of this generalization.

» Following the price freeze of Phase IV of the President's anti-inflation program in early summer 1973, Allan W. Ostar, executive director of the American Association of State Colleges and Universities, wrote a long letter[1] to John T. Dunlop, director, Cost of Living Council, indicating the chaotic effect the price order would have on summer school tuitions—many of which in AASCU's membership had been set by state legislatures only weeks earlier.

» The United States Supreme Court in December 1974 heard oral arguments in the copyright infringement case filed by Williams and Wilkins Company, publisher of medical jour-

1. July 5, 1973.

nals, against two federal libraries, seeking damages for duplicating and distributing numerous articles from the journals. An amici curiae brief was filed for the defendant by the Association of Research Libraries, Medical Library Association, American Association of Law Libraries, Association of American Universities, American Medical Association, American Dental Association, American Association of Dental Schools, the dean of the Faculty of Medicine of Harvard Medical School, the University of Michigan Medical School, American Sociological Association, Modern Language Association of America, and History of Science Society.

» The National Association of Elementary School Principals, National Association of Secondary School Principals, American Association of School Administrators, National Association of State Boards of Education, Council of Chief State School Officers, and National School Boards Association directed "the attention of Congress and the Administration to the proliferation of state and local advisory and management bodies mandated under federal education legislation which, in many instances, duplicate constitutional and statutory educational agencies already existing at state and local levels."[2]

» The National Audio-Visual Association, Inc., made up mainly of audio-visual equipment dealers, lashed out at the concept of "central purchasing," being considered by fifteen states, on the grounds that it could put most of the NAVA members out of business.[3]

» The National Student Lobby attacked the Civil Aeronautics Board for discontinuance of discount youth fares on airlines.[4]

2. *School Administrator*, February 1973, p. 11.
3. *Education U.S.A.*, Jan. 29, 1973.
4. *Change*, October 1972, p. 62.

» The National School Boards Association opposed federal regulation of collective bargaining in the field of education.[5]

» Educators protested a shift of General Services Administration policy which formerly allowed recipients of federal grants to obtain federal excess property for use in furtherance of a federal grant. (GSA cancelled the order under pressure from eighteen trade associations, saying that it put government in a position competitive with local small businesses.)[6]

» The National Association of State Universities and Land-Grant Colleges and the American Association of State Colleges and Universities, in joint release, protested that "state colleges and universities stand to lose between $250 and $300 million in annual income if adult status and voting rights for college-age citizens make non-resident tuition charges inapplicable for the majority of out-of-state students."[7]

» The National Association of Biology Teachers led a fight against a California state law requiring "creation theory" to be included along with "evolution theory" in biology textbooks.[8]

» The American Association for the Advancement of Science called for the elimination of the affidavit (loyalty oath) required by Section 1001(f) of the National Defense Education Act.[9]

These items are a tiny sample only. Beasties lurk throughout the policy jungle. Sometimes, as in many of the cases noted

5. Statement of the National School Boards Association before the Special Labor Subcommittee, U.S. House of Representatives, July 10, 1972.

6. See Agenda, Committee on Governmental Relations, National Association of College and University Business Officers, March 21, 1974, pp. 3–5.

7. Press release, Sept. 25, 1972.

8. NABT News and Notes, October 1972.

9. AAAS Resolution, Dec. 30, 1957.

above, the issue is precise and transient. At other times the issue
is elusive and attenuated. Take, for example, the perennial case
of tax reform. It is widely recognized that existing tax laws
allow the very rich to take advantage of various tax loopholes
and to escape without paying taxes commensurate with their
wealth. This is patently inequitable. But attempts to close such
loopholes, unless extreme care is exercised, can have the perverse
effect of drying up philanthropic gifts to colleges and universities. Private institutions could be mortally affected by ill-con-
sidered changes in tax policy. Even prestigious public institutions
could be hurt badly. In consequence, the administration's tax
recommendations are monitored by higher education associations
with agonizing care. So are the tax views of key congressional
leaders and of the expert staffs of the Joint Committee on Internal Revenue Taxation.

Similarly, changes in spending authorizations, appropriations,
and allotments are followed with particular and continuing concern. During the 1960s, federal spending for education increased
more than fortyfold. Once such monies are on the books, education associations do everything within their power to protect or
increase the level of support. In the late 1960s and early 1970s,
the level of support dropped, first as a result of the Vietnam
war and then because the fiscal dividend came to a precipitate
end (that is, traditionally, federal revenues have increased more
sharply than the growth in the GNP that produced them—a
pattern that changed). With these elements at work, the gap
between federal authorizations and the monies actually appropriated or allotted to educational programs became greater and
greater. Educational associations banded together in an Emergency Committee for the Full Funding of Education Programs
aimed at reducing the gap between authorizations and appropriations. This same committee later cooperated with individual
states and institutions in the largely successful fight against the
Presidential impoundment of education money actually appro-

priated. Meanwhile, many separate educational institutions and associations fought discrete battles over cutbacks that affected specific academic interests: research, professional training, foreign language and area studies, and so on. As Kenneth H. Ashworth, then vice-chancellor for academic affairs of the University of Texas, put it, "If the power to tax is the power to destroy, we might also say that the power to provide financial assistance may become the power to destroy. It is possible that in the years ahead, if institutions let themselves become heavily dependent upon Federal aid, the Federal government may be in a position to practice a form of educational euthanasia by withholding such aid."[10] Ashworth was, in fact, referring not to the future but to a very painful present.

Favorable Rules and Resources

The other side of the shield of "protection from harm" is "favorable consideration," that is, the securing of laws, regulations, interpretations, guidelines, and money that confer some kind of positive benefit upon a particular or the general clientele. In the case of educational interests, sought-after benefits may be grouped into four somewhat overlapping categories: financial, categorical-programmatic, professional, and administrative.

1. *Financial.* Ninety percent of elementary and secondary education and 75 percent of higher education in the United States are publicly supported. As already noted, most of the public money for education has been state and local rather than federal in origin. Over the past twenty years, however, as the demands for and costs of education have skyrocketed, inexorable local pressures have induced larger and larger sums of money to be appropriated at successively higher levels of government. In addition, until recently at least, federal policy-makers have seen

10. *New York Times*, Jan. 22, 1973.

in education generally and in university-based research particularly the possibility of finding answers to pressing national problems: defense, space exploration, health, energy, ecology, urban pathology. Finally, Lyndon Johnson wished to be known as "the Education President," and placed his substantial influence behind federal policies aimed at the federal support of American education—prekindergarten through graduate school.

As a result of all of these forces, there are now on the federal books more than a hundred categorical programs designed to provide financial assistance to various parts and functions of American education. This financial assistance takes the form of grants, loans, construction funds, contracts, and underwriting guaranties. Over forty federal agencies are involved in administering these various funds.

To suggest that most of the $16 billion of the federal budget available annually to education got there through the work of education interest groups would be a gross distortion. Presidential and congressional leadership, Sputnik and the Vietnam war, and a host of what Charles Beard called "secular drifts" may explain the size of the federal education budget better than do any conscious petitions by groups of educational clientele. The work of the latter should not, however, be underevaluated. Increasingly, partnerships have been formed between education interest groups and the political and bureaucratic leadership in the executive and legislative branches in the determination of spending targets. The Committee for Full Funding of Educational Programs has had an important influence on educational appropriations in recent years, perhaps as great as $5 billion above Presidential recommendations. And the pressures by group interests have not slackened. Even on cursory review, the platforms and programs of education associations reveal their constant concern with federal financial aid to education. Note the following items drawn at random from recent years:

» The Policies Commission of the Council for Exceptional Children called upon the federal government to give categorical support to exceptional children (handicapped, gifted) including money to train teachers of the handicapped.[11]

» The "Big Six" (National Association of Elementary School Principals, National Association of Secondary School Principals, American Association of School Administrators, National Association of State Boards of Education, Council of Chief State School Officers, National School Boards Association) called for "adequate funding of existing programs" and for moving the federal government's share of the total cost of elementary and secondary education to at least one-third.[12]

» The Council of Chief State School Officers endorsed federal assumption of one-third of the cost of elementary and secondary education and called for increased federal funds for state administration of federal programs.[13]

» National School Boards Association called for 40 percent of costs of K–12 to be borne by the federal government.[14]

» Of the twelve votes (six in the House, six in the Senate) monitored by NEA for their 1971–72 "Legislative Report Card," nine were targeted at financial assistance to education.

» The American Council on Education, joined by seven other organizations, asked Congress to approve increases totaling nearly $648 million over the administration's budget for higher education programs in the U.S. Office of Education in the 1975 fiscal year starting July 1, 1974. Testimony was

11. Council for Exceptional Children Assembly, 1972.
12. *School Administrator*, February 1973, p. 11.
13. CCSSO *Stateline*, Fall 1972.
14. Statement of the National School Boards Association before the Special Labor Subcommittee, U.S. House of Representatives, July 19, 1972.

presented in two parts to the House Appropriations Subcommittee on the Departments of Labor and Health, Education, and Welfare.[15]

» Impacted Area Schools called for full funding of Public Laws 815 and 874.[16]

The form in which the money comes and the discretionary channels through which it flows are, as noted below, at times as important as the volume itself. But any look at the federal policy agenda of education associations discloses the central concern with financial support.

2. *Categorical-programmatic.* One might argue that categorical programs are simply the substantive side of "financial." In many cases this is true, but there are substantial exceptions. For more than a hundred years, for example, bills have been introduced in the Congress for "general aid" to education. Although a large general aid bill has never been enacted, smaller and quasi-general aid bills have. Two of the most popular series of education laws, those dealing with aid to impacted areas and those providing grants and loans directly to college students (GI Bill, Basic Opportunity Grants, National Defense [later Direct] Student Loans, etc.) come close in conception to being general aid acts. Even the Elementary-Secondary Education Act of 1965, targeted on the needs of the children of the poor, was interpreted by many school districts as a form of general aid. The attempts of the higher education community to obtain substantial federal money for "institutional aid" during the struggles over the Education Amendments of 1972 were really a plea for "general aid." Finally, the Nixon administration's concept of "special revenue sharing" for education, at the very least an attempt at

15. *Higher Education and National Affairs,* May 17, 1974, p. 1.
16. Impacted Area Schools Information Service, Bulletin #12, Oct. 23, 1972.

program consolidation, moved semantically in the direction of general aid (let state and local authorities determine how education money should be spent). Actually, half of the Nixon administration's general revenue sharing funds since 1973 ended up in education, and thereby qualify as a kind of general federal aid to education.

Many education associations, however, are interested in particular categories of federal assistance—money targeted for special educational programs: the handicapped, the disadvantaged, vocational education, foreign language study, international student exchanges, drug education, rehabilitation, health training, agricultural extension services, educational research and development, classroom and laboratory construction, adult and continuing education—the list goes on and on. Around each of these there develops a cluster of associations intent on securing special governmental support for the program in question. Again, a few random items will illuminate the emphasis on categorical programs:

» The Council for Exceptional Children wanted a "national information service to bring about effective coordination of services and research efforts" for the gifted and the handicapped.[17]

» The National Student Lobby wanted federal support for child care centers on campuses.[18]

» The Association for Educational Communications and Technology was concerned, in 1972, about three educational programs sponsored by Congress: title III of NDEA, title VI of the Higher Education Act, and parts C and D of the Education Professions Development Act. Each of these was targeted on support for educational technology.[19]

17. Council for Exceptional Children Assembly, 1972.
18. National Student Lobby, Flier for Second Annual Convention, 1972.
19. Testimony before the Senate Appropriations Subcommittee handling

» The National Council of Teachers of Mathematics and the Mathematical Association of America have formed a loose coalition to advance the cause of the metric system.[20]

» The Association for Supervision and Curriculum Development (NEA) urged that 20 percent of cable television channels be reserved for education and public affairs programs.[21]

» The American Vocational Association backed renewal of the Manpower Development and Training Act.[22]

Some education interests do not confine their attention to matters that are strictly educational. This is understandable. As noted earlier, a great variety of governmental programs have direct or indirect effects on educational institutions and processes. So the chief state school officers backed the eighteen-year-old vote; so the National Student Lobby called for a curtailment of the President's war powers.

3. *Professional.* Much of the energy of education associations is poured into the development and protection of professional status and privilege. This takes many forms: attempts to be included in or, as Sam Goldwyn put it, to be "included out," that is, attempts to restrict membership and otherwise to define eligibility; attempts to gain advantage in bargaining situations; attempts to protect autonomies, freedoms, and perquisites; attempts to improve salaries, pensions, and fringe benefits. Several recent items are illustrative:

Departments of Labor and of Health, Education, and Welfare funds, July 17, 1974.

20. Interview by James Browne with James D. Gates, executive secretary, NCTM, Jan. 22, 1973.

21. ASCD, *Interpretations*, Occasional paper, November 1971.

22. Resolution #6 passed by House of Delegates, Dec. 5, 1973, AVA Convention, Atlanta, Ga.

» A coalition of the National Education Association and the American Federation of State, County and Municipal Employees lobbied for a "federal collective bargaining law for public employees (including teachers) modeled along the lines of the National Labor Relations Act."[23]

» The Council on Hotel, Restaurant and Institutional Education wanted more professional training in the area of food, lodging, and food service to be sponsored by the Department of Defense and other government agencies such as the Bureau of Indian Affairs.[24]

» Various educational groups backed a "Mobile Teacher Retirement Assistance Act," providing for the vesting of pension rights in the teachers themselves rather than in a particular school district.[25]

» The Council of Chief State School Officers called for a "performance based" certification of teachers.[26]

» The National Association of Elementary School Principals urged "legal recognition" of the elementary school principalship, and called for "not less than a master's degree and a successful teaching experience in elementary schools" as minimum qualifications for the job. NAESP also stressed "professional unity," decrying—by implication—the division of education into "teachers" and "administrators."[27]

23. NEA, "Summary of Legislative Action, 92nd Congress" (1973).

24. Letter to Stephen K. Bailey from Richard M. Landmark, executive vice-president, Council on Hotel, Restaurant and Institutional Education, Jan. 5, 1973.

25. See, for example, Council of Chief State School Officers, *Policies and Resolutions*, adopted at Annual Business Meeting, Louisville, Ky., Nov. 17, 1971, and National Association of Elementary School Principals, *Resolutions*, 1972.

26. CCSSO, *Policies and Resolutions*, 1971.

27. NAESP, *Resolutions*, 1972.

» The Association of American Publishers testified before the House Judiciary Committee in favor of a bill to protect writers from subpeonas that would force them to disclose the information they gather and its source.[28]

» The American Civil Liberties Union brought lawsuits in a "war on secrecy"—actions on behalf of recognized scholars who wish to conduct research in government files that have been improperly classified.[29]

» The Association of American Medical Colleges wanted legislation that would broaden federal support for the education and training of family practitioners to include "all specialities" providing primary care.[30]

» The American Psychological Association wanted all health care plans to recognize the mental health aspects of disease and of research related to disease.[31]

One case deserves recounting, for it is prototypical of attempts by organizations and associations to redefine the professional status of their membership and their clientele. It relates how the United Business Schools Association (now the Association of Independent Colleges and Schools) labored over the years to have proprietary schools and students included in legislative definitions of eligibility for certain kinds of federal educational aid. My interview with the AICS executive director, Richard A. Fulton, led to a request for a written summary of how this significant shift had taken place. What follows is a slightly edited and abbreviated version of Fulton's response.

28. Statement of Kenneth D. McCormick before Subcommittee No. 3 of the Committee on Judiciary, U.S. House of Representatives, Sept. 27, 1972.

29. Letter to the Editor, *New York Times*, Dec. 22, 1972.

30. AAMC, *Annual Report, 1971–72*, p. 9.

31. "Psychology and National Health Care," *American Psychologist*, November 1971.

Any chronology of the legislative inclusion of proprietary schools or students really must run on three parallel but independent tracks.

Track A: Higher Education

This story begins with the 1958 National Defense Education Act. In NDEA's Title II, a system of student loans for scientific students was laid out. To be eligible, it was provided that a student must be attending a "non-profit" (i.e. non-proprietary) four-year educational institution.

In 1964, students in two-year accredited non-profit terminal programs were allowed to qualify for NDSL loans.

Also in 1964, the Morse Committee in the Senate reported favorably a bill authorizing a system of insured loans with subsidized interest. The definition of an eligible institution was broad enough to include an accredited proprietary institution. It removed the non-profit element from the definition.

In 1965, S. 600 proposed a system of subsidized insured loans. Included was access to those loans for students in accredited proprietary schools. When this was finally enacted late in the year as the National Vocational Student Loan Insurance Act under the leadership of Congressman John Dent, this marked the first USOE administered program available on a broad base to students in accredited proprietary schools.

In 1968, the Higher Education Amendments expanded access to the College Work-Study Program and to the National Defense Student Loan Program by permitting them to be made available to students in accredited proprietary schools. In that Act, Section 461 (b) was drafted defining a "proprietary institution of higher education." This has been carried forward to the present Section 491 (b).

Thus in 1972, the expansion of the student aid programs to include Equal Opportunity Grants and Basic Opportunity Grants for students in proprietary schools required no new definition. The definition was written in 1968. It merely meant that the two remaining programs were now available to students in proprietary schools. . . . the Congress of the United States has made a policy pronouncement legitimating proprietary education . . . an example is the mandate of the composition of the State Planning Commissions under Section 1202 [of the Education Amendments Act of 1972].

Track B: Vocational Education Act

In 1963 Congress enacted the Vocational Education Act. In that Act there was clear language authorizing vocational education "under contract." In addition to the language there was clear congressional intent via the floor debate in both the House and the Senate.

Nevertheless, in 1968 when testifying before the Pucinski subcommittee UBSA challenged the USOE to cite a single instance of a single student being educated in a single school with a single dollar authorized under the Vocational Education Act of 1963 through "under contract" training. No evidence was forthcoming. The USOE always referred to MDTA [Manpower and Development Training Act] training but they never could cite Voc-ed money.

In 1968, the Vocational Education Act was amended to amplify and clarify the authority. The authority had been there since 1963.

Track C: MDTA and Vocation Rehabilitation

Since 1921 students have been trained under contract with federal and state funds in proprietary schools pursuant to the Vocational Rehabilitation Program. The Vocational Rehabilitation Act neither authorizes nor forbids such "under contract" activity. It has just been a long-standing practice.

In 1962, the Manpower Development and Training Act was passed. The early days of the MDTA under USOE administration exhibited the institutional complex of those charged with implementing the program. Every effort was made to exclude the utilization of proprietary schools.

The Act was persistently amended in 1963, (probably in '64 and '65 as well), to expand the authority of the Secretary of HEW to overcome this reluctance of both federal and state administrators to contract with proprietary schools.

By and large, there is now a degree of appreciable acceptance.[32]

This extended description of the struggle of proprietary institutions for eligibility under various federal education programs is a dramatic illustration of a common phenomenon. If there are benefits to be distributed, education interests do everything within their power to see that the definition of eligibility is large

32. Letter to Stephen K. Bailey from Richard H. Fulton, Jan. 18, 1973.

enough to include them. As a result of Fulton's quiet but persistent work over a number of years in relation to a variety of federal programs, the list of postsecondary institutions eligible for federal educational assistance has moved from 2,500 a few years back to nearly 4,000 today.

4. *Administrative.* A careful review of the newsletters, annual reports, and policy proclamations issued by education associations quickly reveals their continuing interest in the administration of whatever programs are on the books. Their concern is sound. The way in which programs are administered—including the locus of discretionary judgments about the allocation of program resources—is a matter of grave concern to key actors in the drama of intergovernmental relations. In this context, for example, President Nixon's recommendations for revenue sharing became important issues of financial administration to the affected education community. The question, Is revenue sharing good or bad for education? is meaningless unless qualified to include the related questions, What kind of revenue sharing? and What levels of administration will determine its final targets? It might be argued that if federal revenue is shared with states rather than directly with localities, thereby lodging the spending discretion at the state level, then revenue sharing is a good thing for states. But what does this mean? If by "states" we mean state education departments, then chief state school officers should be happy. But what if "states" means governors and legislative leaders, and what if these august officials happen not to think highly of education as a state priority?

Or what happens if the administration's proposal for special revenue sharing is adopted by the Congress—a program of grant consolidation, allowing substantial state and local leeway in determining the allocation of funds within the field of education? If troubled city school districts are short-changed in these allocation decisions, urban-based and big-city school superin-

tendents, teachers organizations, and parents groups are likely
to be dissatisfied with the locus of administrative discretion.
The concerns that education interest groups have for program
administration are wide and varied. Once again a few items from
the recent past will illuminate the issue:

» The National University Extension Association wanted "more
   permanent funding of federal higher continuing education
   programs at colleges and universities in lieu of uncertain, ad
   hoc, annual project funding."[33]

» The Big Six urged the enactment of FY'74 educational appropriations *before July 1973* (in order to give their constituents time to plan for the opening of school in the fall).[34]

» The Big Six urged the enactment of legislation to enable
   state and local agencies to develop procedures to improve
   education for all children "without being stifled by excessive
   federal regulations."[35]

» The Council of Chief State School Officers was upset about
   being bypassed in a new desegregation aid program. Chiefs
   believed *they* should choose the 500 school districts which
   would participate in the new federal program to reduce racial
   isolation. Fred Burke, then Commissioner of Education in
   Rhode Island, commented, "USOE say we are supposed to
   master plan, but how can we when USOE deals directly with
   local school districts?"[36]

» The National Association of Elementary School Principals
   called for more federal support and also for more flexibility
   in allocating money.[37]

33. NUEA, *Newsletter*, April 21, 1972.
34. *School Administrator*, February 1973, p. 11.
35. Ibid.
36. "Washington Monitor," *Education U.S.A.*, Nov. 22, 1972.
37. NAESP, *Resolutions*, 1972.

» The American Vocational Association wanted bureau status for vocational education within the U.S. Office of Education (thereby increasing, in administrative terms, the power and prestige of the voc-ed programs).[38]

» The National School Boards Association wanted direct representation on the Advisory Commission on Intergovernmental Relations (a research and consultative body created by federal statute to make policy recommendations in the field of federal-state-local relations).[39]

» Speakers at the Association of American Colleges meeting in San Francisco claimed that "more and more presidents and deans at institutions across the country report that the traditional autonomy of colleges and universities is being eroded by decisions made by state and federal office holders."[40]

» The Association of American Medical Colleges believed that federal aid programs "should not dictate the *organization of programs* within the medical schools" (emphasis supplied).[41]

» The Council of Chief State School Officers wanted prior formal consultation by USOE with groups of chiefs formed by the Council *before* legislative guidelines and regulations or budgetary initiatives were taken by USOE that would significantly affect state education interests.[42]

In the higher education community, no administrative issue in recent years has created more soul searching or more genuine frustration than the attempt of the federal government to induce

38. Resolution #4 passed by House of Delegates, Dec. 6, 1972, AVA Convention, Chicago, Ill.

39. NSBA statement before the Special Labor Subcommittee, U.S. House of Representatives, July 10, 1972.

40. *New York Times*, Jan. 22, 1973.

41. AAMC, *Annual Report*, 1971–72, p. 9.

42. CCSSO, *Stateline*, Fall 1972.

ethnic and sex equality in higher education personnel practices through "affirmative action." Federal regulations and guidelines have said in effect that no postsecondary educational institution would be eligible for federal funds unless it could demonstrate a bona fide attempt to increase the percentage of women and minorities on its faculty and in its administrative staff. The clash of perspectives between bureaucrats and educators about the meaning of title ix of the 1972 Education Amendments is still going on: When has affirmative action in fact taken place? What constitutes a "qualified" person? Who should be able to look at personnel files that have traditionally been guarded? What constitutes an unwise invasion of the autonomies and immunities of universities and colleges?

The Issue of Intensity

One final caveat must be noted. A simple listing of stated policy objectives conveys a false sense of reality. For most education associations, their list of stated policy goals is a complex code that needs constant deciphering. Some items are there, not because of any likelihood that they are achievable in the proximate future, but because an important minority in the association feels strongly about the issue. Other items are included because an important ally of the association believes them to be important. Some goals are trial balloons and are floated with the expectation that they may be shot down. A few items may be ballast to be sacrificed if they impede the ascendancy of more important balloons. In short, there may be a vast variety of political explanations for the ordering and nuances of the various planks in the policy platforms of an education association.

At any one time, only a few issues are truly crucial. To find out what education associations really want, it is more important to watch what they do than what they print: actions truly speak louder than formal words in delineating what interest groups actually believe to be important.

CHAPTER FOUR

Relations with Government

WE NOW TURN to the strategy and tactics of influence. Regrettably, one important aspect of this phenomenon must, in this brief guide, be largely ignored: the courts. Anyone who reviews the national policy developments in education over the past few decades is impressed by the major role played by the judicial branch of our various levels of government in shaping educational directions. Education issues involving civil rights, church-state relations, equitable finance, student rights, faculty due process, collective bargaining, and a host of other matters have been argued before the nation's tribunals. Litigation has frequently been initiated or supported by education associations—particularly in the form of amicus curiae briefs. The slow rituals of the legal process have a grace and dignity usually lacking in the rough and tumble of executive and legislative combat. But behind the scenes, education interest groups and their attorneys fight for their side on judicial issues quite as diligently as they do on matters before the other two branches. The techniques are different; constraints of tradition and judicial independence preclude personal contacts and maximize attention to formal argument. For the most part, education groups give less attention to following court cases than to watching closely developments within the administration and the Congress. But powerful and costly education battles have been and will continue to be waged before the judiciary, for the courts are impressive instruments in the shaping of educational policy.

The "Lobbying" Dilemma

As noted in chapter 1, relationships between education associations, on the one hand, and the Congress and the administration on the other are, with important exceptions, carried on somewhat nervously within the context of Section 501(c)(3) of the Internal Revenue Code. In essence, Section 501(c)(3) permits an organization or association to claim tax exemption if it is not an "action" organization, that is, if no substantial part of its activities (5 percent or less, according to one IRS decision) is devoted to carrying on propaganda, otherwise attempting to influence legislation, or intervening in any political campaign on behalf of any candidate for public office. Internal Revenue Service regulations compiled in 1971 give the following interpretation to these strictures:

An organization is an "action" organization if a substantial part of its activities is attempting to influence legislation by propaganda or otherwise. For this purpose, an organization will be regarded as attempting to influence legislation if the organization:
(a) Contacts, or urges the public to contact, members of the legislative body for the purpose of proposing, supporting, or opposing legislation; or
(b) Advocates the adoption or rejection of legislation.[1]

Inasmuch as there are some seventeen or more categories of tax-exempt organizations, most of which are not subject to lobbying constraints, the question arises, Why do most educational associations incorporate under the one provision of the Code which expressly prohibits substantial lobbying? The answer is that Section 501(c)(3) organizations may receive donations that are tax deductible to the donor or are acceptable to IRS without endangering the tax status of contributing educational institutions or private foundations like the Ford Foundation, the W. K. Kellogg Foundation, or the Carnegie Corporation of

1. *The Washington Lobby* (Washington: Congressional Quarterly, 1971), p. 95.

New York—foundations that have been major benefactors of some of the key education associations. A few education associations have indeed incorporated under the "Business League" section of the Code, 501(c)(6), a section that permits tax exemption for the organization and contains no prohibition against lobbying. Donors to Section 501(c)(6) organizations, however, may not claim tax deductions for their gifts, nor may private institutions and foundations make contributions and grants to such organizations without jeopardizing their own tax-exempt status.

Whatever the reasons for seeking Section 501(c)(3) status, education associations enjoying such status find themselves in the uncomfortable position of "influencing" without "lobbying," of "providing information" without "propaganda." Hairsplitting and subterfuge are constant. Every Section 501(c)(3) education association worth its salt cares about the direction and fate of legislative proposals that affect its clientele. And they work in a variety of ways to influence such legislation. But they skirt the 501(c)(3) prohibitions with the skill of a firebird. A few, inadvertently perhaps, violate the Code. But of scores of letters received in response to a general inquiry in the winter of 1972–73, all but a few associations included a sentence similar to, or identical with, the following: "[this association] is not a lobbying organization, although we often send out materials to congressmen at *their* request."

In addition to this general claim, the concatenation of rationalizations included the following:

Only an insubstantial part of the association's activities is devoted to propaganda and lobbying.

The association provides congressmen with data only, not propaganda or advocacy.

The association's interest is not with a particular piece of legislation but with the principle *underlying* the legislation.

The association's newsletters provide *information* to the members; if the members wish to approach their representatives, it is up to them. The association's reaction is to the President's program, not to its legislative implementation.

NEA has attempted to clarify the issue by reregistering as a 501(c)(6) Business League Organization and then creating a separate 501(c)(3) foundation called the National Foundation for the Improvement of Education—a small research institute.

For most of the education associations, the existing pattern of incorporation is worrisome. At the very least, it blunts energies in areas of activity that are close to an education association's reason for being; at the worst, it subjects education associations to accusations of hypocrisy. Part of the story that follows involves activities that raise doubts about the legal proprieties of many education association activities. In my judgment, many education associations would be better off if they followed the NEA compromise or incorporated under other kinds of tax-exempt provisions of the Internal Revenue Code, or joined with the Coalition of Concerned Charities in urging appropriate amendments to Section 501(c)(3) to permit "grass roots" lobbying.

Relations with the Executive Branch

The Internal Revenue Code makes no reference to attempts of Section 501(c)(3) associations to influence executive branch policies. This would seem to leave the field open. Yet most education associations have no real feel for dealing with the executive branch, at least at high levels of macro-policy such as budgets and program priorities that have far-reaching effects. During the Johnson administration, communication was almost too easy: proeducation officials initiated calls *to* the associations. During most of the Nixon administration, the problem was quite the reverse. Associations were frustrated by White House, Office of Management and Budget (OMB), and HEW policy-

baffles that conveyed a strong sense that education was not a high-priority item on the agenda of tight federal budgets. Exercising a questionable constitutional power in questionable ways, President Nixon attempted time and again to impound funds appropriated by the Congress for educational functions. Courts almost unanimously held that if the underlying authorizations were tied to specific congressional entitlements (as opposed to discretionary funds that could be spent according to the canons of administrative discretion), impoundment by the President was unconstitutional. Still, the sense of Presidential priorities was clearly communicated by impoundment gestures, and some weakly defended appropriations were in fact stalled. At this writing, the experience with the Ford administration is too limited to reveal a clear pattern.

In order to understand the frustrations of education associations in dealing with the executive branch on matters of general (as distinct from detailed or highly categorical) policy, it is necessary to recall education's place(s) in the executive branch structure. A few years ago, Representative Edith Green reported that more that forty federal departments and agencies were involved in educational policies and programs. Recently these have included preeminently the Office of Education and the National Institute of Education in the Education Division of the Department of Health, Education, and Welfare. But major educational activities are carried out by the Department of Defense, the National Science Foundation, the Veterans Administration, the Department of State, the National Endowment for the Humanities, the National Institutes of Health, the Department of Labor, the Department of Agriculture, and the Federal Communications Commission—to name but a few of the obvious agencies. There is no place short of the Executive Office of the President for coordinating and rationalizing these various educational programs—even on paper. A lame attempt to create and foster a Federal Interagency Committee on Education (FICE) was started in the mid-1960s and continues to this day under the chairmanship of the Assistant Secretary of HEW for Education. But FICE suffers the weakness of most interagency committees that are subject matter rich and power poor.

In this complex universe, educational policy initiatives that begin to stir at a series of low bureaucratic levels must run a vertical gantlet past a series of superordinates, none of whom has education as his major concern. Education is not the major interest of the Secretary of Defense, or the Administrator of Veterans Affairs, or the Secretary of Agriculture. Education is not always a major interest of the Secretary of Health, Education, and Welfare, whose budget for health and welfare is many times larger than his budget for education. Furthermore, if education is a low priority in the Executive Office of the President or is seen primarily as a state and local function to be supported, if at all, by federal funds through general or special revenue sharing, this reality is communicated downward in a variety of ways and informs and conditions subordinate discretions.

One reason education associations have pressed for a Cabinet-level department for education is their realization that, once matters of policy and budget recommendations go beyond the level of the HEW Assistant Secretary for Education, there lies a rocky path past the Assistant Secretary, Comptroller; Assistant Secretary (Planning and Evaluation); Assistant Secretary (Legislation); Under Secretary; Secretary; Office of Management and Budget; and White House. There is no high-level federal spokesman for education except by accident of special Presidential interest. HEW's Assistant Secretaries for Education and Commissioners of Education do their best to be friends of American education, but time and again their programs and policy recommendations are modified or abolished by policy-planners or cost/benefit-minded budget analysts who enjoy the confidence of the Secretary of HEW or of key White House aides to the President.

The state of the art of measuring the effectiveness of educational programs is not high. Moreover, many of the key benefits of education are likely to continue to elude the sophisticated measures of quantity-oriented program analysts and evaluators. In the executive agencies, therefore, there is an almost built-in management bias against educational programs, which cannot compete in terms of hard measurements with "miles of highways" laid or "acres of soy beans" planted.

For the education associations, whose major instruments of persuasion have been, not hard data and quantitative analysis, but the rhetoric of faith and the warmth of personal contact, most of the machinery of executive branch policy making seems as forbidding as it is inaccessible. Of more than sixty association officials interviewed in the winter of 1972–73, only two admitted of direct contact with the Secretary level in HEW or with key advisers in the Executive Office of the President. When approaches to top executive branch officials were deemed imperative, most association representatives went through friends on Capitol Hill—especially minority (Republican) legislators or their staffs. But even this tactic had limited utility, at least during the period when Haldeman and Ehrlichman growled at Presidential friends and foes alike.

As we shall see, all this does not mean that education associations have had no traffic with executive agencies. It only means that in recent years communication has tended to be limited to matters of program implementation and evaluation that can be handled at the bureau level and below, rather than to matters of overall budgets and program priorities that are handled at the departmental level and above.

The Information Symbiosis

Education associations are key intermediaries in an information network that provides clients and members with material about federal agency programs and that provides federal agencies with operational feedback. The alliance between agencies and associations is frequently a love-hate relationship. The agencies and the associations need each other, but the symbiosis is troubled by the agencies' beliefs that associations want money without accountability, and by the associations' beliefs that agencies suffer from what the late Wallace B. Sayre called "the triumph of technique over purpose."

The symbiosis is most effective when both an agency bureau and an association benefit from cooperative attempts to get out the word to the professional grass roots. The "word" may be a new regulation or a guideline delineating the fine points of a new program, a notice of change in procedures for grant applications, a new interpretation of eligibility for an old program. Whatever the piece of information, the agency benefits from a communications network that is infinitely more precise and direct than the public media, which may not even carry the information because "it lacks newsworthiness." And the numerous federal agency press releases mailed directly to schools and districts often get buried in the in-baskets of harried administrators, where they remain "pending." Newsletters from education associations, however, are frequently read faithfully. Their readers assume that the government handouts have been winnowed and that what remains is significant to them and their problems.

In addition, association Washington offices keep their telephone lines humming. A cryptic newspaper reference to a new program or a changed policy may well prompt a call from the executive director of a Washington association requesting elaboration or clarification. Some Washington offices of education associations maintain voluminous files on federal grants, contracts, requests for proposals (known in the trade as "RFP's"), regulations, guidelines, legislation, laws, statistics, and pronouncements. For example, the federal program files of the American Association of State Colleges and Universities represent the most comprehensive and usable set of data available on higher education policies and projects. At levels K–12, NEA is in part a vast reference library which can be tapped at any time by its diverse membership.

A few concrete examples of the information-dispensing function may point up some of the generalities noted above:

» The National University Extension Association *Newsletter* of April 21, 1972, told its readers that "in its survey of higher continuing educational programs of the Federal Government, the [National Advisory] Council [on Extension and Continuing Education] identified 143 separate programs which, in whole or in part, provide funds for university extension, continuing education and community service activities."

» In a memo of February 1, 1972, Dr. John A. D. Cooper, of the Association of American Medical Colleges, wrote to his Council of Deans that the "Cost of Living Council announced January 26 that tuition fees and other charges of private, nonprofit schools, colleges, and universities were exempt from price controls under Phase II."[2]

» Frank Mensel, then legislative director for the American Association of Community and Junior Colleges, praised North Carolina for having "picked up support from some forty different Federal programs, ranging from the Appalachian and Coastal Plains Commission and the Public Works sections of the Economic Development Act to the National Aeronautics and Space Act and the National Foundation on the Arts and Humanities."[3]

Almost every association's newsletter contains program information that the government is interested in having reach the

2. From AAMC papers made available to the author, winter 1973.
3. R. Frank Mensel, "Federal Programs: A Stimulus for Educational Development," in Occasional Paper #17 (Los Angeles: University of California, Los Angeles, 1972).

grass roots or which the association's Washington headquarters believes is of significance to its readership.

In addition, association conferences and conventions serve as useful forums for government officials, who are often asked to speak or to serve on panels.

The other side of the coin is, of course, the flow of information and opinion back from the grass roots through the association to the Washington agency. At times, this relationship is formal: association officials are asked to serve on ad hoc or statutory advisory committees to bureaus or programs. At other times, a government program director will ask an association to sample its members for opinions on the reasonableness of a prepared guideline or regulation. Or again, associations will take the initiatve in bringing complaints or fears to the attention of executive branch officials—through comments and newsletters or through direct contact by letter, telephone, or personal invitation. The following illustrations give some sense of the variety of messages sent from or through Washington associations to federal officials:

»   "The Office of Education has announced the planned development of an integrated Federal state statistical system called the Common Core of Data for the 70's (CCD-'70). William A. Goddard, Executive Director of NATTS [National Association of Trade and Technical Schools] has been invited by Don Davies, Deputy Commissioner of Development, USOE, to serve on the steering group to develop data requirements, procedures, and mechanisms of CCD-'70."[4]

»   The policy statement of the National Association of College and University Business Officers approved in May 1972 reported that "with regard to the administrative programs of government executive agencies, the Association and the

4. NATTS *News*, December 1972.

Committee on Governmental Relations make themselves available, through their staff representatives, for consultation on policies or regulations touching the administration of federal programs at colleges and universities. Such contacts are direct and they are conducted routinely as a means of encouraging helpful communications between the federal agencies and the institutions on problems of management."[5]

» The Federal Trade Commission has sought testimony from the American Personnel and Guidance Association in revising proposed guidelines relating to private trade and technical schools.[6]

» NUEA *Newsletter* of April 21, 1972, criticized the annual report of the National Advisory Council on Extension and Continuing Education for its unwillingness to give up "project proposal" methods of awarding funds for a model based more closely on the "cooperative extension" experience.

» The Council of Chief State School Officers, noting the strengthening of USOE regional officers, commented: "recognizing that some USOE activities make it desirable for Federal personnel to be located in the state, the Council urges that the U.S. Commissioner of Education deal directly with the Chief State School Officer in each state on matters requiring important administrative decisions in elementary and secondary education."[7]

» CCSSO "sharply criticized the Office of Education for its recent callback of title i funds, alleged to have been misspent by some states, maintaining that no constructive purpose can

5. "NACUBO and Federal Programs Affecting Higher Education: A Statement of Policy," mimeographed (Washington: The Association, July 1973), p. 3.

6. Interview with Charles L. Lewis and Joseph McDonough, Feb. 26, 1973.

7. CCSSO, *Stateline*, Fall 1971.

be served by federal audits of ESEA prior to 1969 and pledging its assistance to state and local districts in resisting the recall of funds."[8]

» "President John B. Geissinger [American Association of School Administrators], with eight other presidents of educational organizations, conferred with President Nixon at the White House on important issues."[9]

» NEA's list of federal agency contacts during the 92nd Congress included the Treasury Department, U.S. Office of Education, Office of Management and Budget, the Department of Labor, National Science Foundation, Department of Defense, Civil Service Commission, Equal Employment Opportunity Commission, the White House, National Archives, Bureau of Indian Affairs, Veterans Administration, Teacher Corps, Department of Housing and Urban Development, Social Security Administration, Internal Revenue Service, Pay Board, Department of Agriculture, General Services Administration, Department of Justice, and Department of Commerce.[10]

» President John A. D. Cooper of the Association of American Medical Colleges expressed concern that most of the top officials in the Department of HEW responsible for federal health programs were being replaced simultaneously.[11]

» The U.S. Office of Education asked the Association of American Universities to comment on the November 24, 1972, working draft of an "issue paper of Task Force on State Postsecondary Education Commissions." AAU responded

8. Ibid.

9. AASA *Annual Report,* 1971–72 (Washington: The Association, n.d.), p. 3.

10. NEA, "Summary of Legislative Action, 92nd Congress" (1973), passim.

11. AAMC *Bulletin,* December 1972.

with a twenty-page, paragraph-by-paragraph set of suggested deletions and corrections. In addition, the heads of six state universities or university systems responded to the same draft, by letter dated December 18, 1972, addressed to John D. Phillips, chairman of the Task Force on State Postsecondary Education Commissions, USOE. The letter noted that the signing educators had "been asked indirectly by Dr. Joseph P. Cosand, Deputy Commissioner for Higher Education, to submit to you our written reactions and comments. . . ." There followed a three-page, single-spaced comment, along with a number of separately attached comments. The signers were: John E. Corbally, Jr., president, University of Illinois; William Friday, president, University System of North Carolina; Charles J. Hitch, president, University of California; Charles A. LeMaistre, chancellor, University of Texas System; C. Brice Ratchford, president, University of Missouri; and John C. Weaver, president, University of Wisconsin.

These few items may give the flavor of the kinds of information feedback to decision-makers that stems from association and institutional activity. It is important for public officials to know where the shoe pinches—or might pinch. The educational associations are not reluctant in providing or forwarding such advice.

The Case of the 2500–2690 MHz

In addition to facilitating a two-way flow of information, some associations play a major, direct role in affecting important aspects of executive branch policy that have a bearing on education. An example of this phenomenon at its best is to be found in the case of the 2500–2690 megahertz.[12] The case recounts the work

12. The case history is paraphrased from a section of *Joint Council on Educational Telecommunications Biannual Report, July 1969–June 1971* (Washington: JCET).

of the Joint Council on Educational Telecommunications in cap-
turing a particular transmission band for a communications satellite launched in May 1973.

JCET is a small organization with a professional staff of one
—Frank Norwood. JCET is supported by a number of education
associations, including NEA and ACE. Its main function is to
follow federal telecommunications policies to make sure that the
telecommunications laws and regulations take into account and
are protective of the interests of education.

In 1969, Norwood learned that the National Aeronautics and
Space Administration planned to launch in May 1973 its Applications Technology Satellite F, which would include two space-
borne television transmitters capable of beaming educational
programs around the world. Norwood learned further that an
interagency decision had already been made to seek a particular
transmission band for this and similar communication satellites.
Such an assignment would have closed forever education's access to the very frequencies essential to the development of a
cost-effective educational satellite service. JCET first called this
discrepancy to the attention of the educational community at a
1969 National Conference on Telecommunications Policy and
Education held, with the help of the Kettering Foundation, at
the University of Georgia. Shortly thereafter, JCET began a
series of filings with the Federal Communications Commission
and accelerated a campaign to alert its own members and the
educational community to the critical need for action.

Had the previously agreed-upon transmission band been re-
tained, it would have required a receiving antenna sixteen feet
wide, priced at $100,000 each. However, a signal operating at
the 2500–2690 MHz band would call for a receiving antenna
less than ten inches in diameter which would cost less than $100
each in large quantities. The implications for educational institutions and individual learners are obvious.

The Federal Communications Commission's initial reaction to

the JCET submissions was that they were "impractical." Finally, at the urging of one commissioner, open hearings were held. JCET provided a series of star witnesses—a list put together at an emergency meeting of education groups called by JCET for the purpose. The testimony turned the U.S. agency's opinion around. Norwood then brought pressure to bear on the U.S. Department of State to present this country's revised position to the World Administrative Radio Conference in Geneva in June 1971. The American delegation included HEW's Dr. Albert Horley, who gained support of many of the Third World's delegation for the 2500 MHz proposal. The conference agreed to allocate the 2500–2690 MHz band to broadcast satellites on a worldwide basis. In two years, the "hopeless cause" of satellites for education had become an affirmative worldwide commitment of a valuable radio spectrum.

Relations with the Congress

As education association people contemplate the Congress, the neat structures remembered from junior high civics almost totally disappear. Occasionally, a moment of high drama occurs on the House or Senate floor when the outcome of the vote on an important piece of legislation is unknown and the attentive interests in the galleries wait anxiously. But such occasions are rare. Normally, if an education legislation observer takes the time to watch the outcome of a floor vote, it is to catch a minute's rest or to congratulate or console a tired ego.

"Congress" to most lobbyists is a half-dozen members and their personal and committee staffs. On the Senate side, because of the great number of committee assignments each member must hold, the impossible demands of subject-matter coverage, and the large constituencies back home, personal and committee staff members who concentrate on education matters tend to have enormous influence. Staff experts like Stephen Wexler, Richard Smith, and Harley M. Dirks, have come close to being

"Surrogate Senators for Education." Education's representatives
deal, on the Senate side, almost totally with staff.

On the House side, real education expertise resides in a
handful of key members. A few House staff members are knowledgeable and powerful, but their bosses are more accessible and
better informed on detail than is generally true on the Senate
side. In consequence, education spokesmen find themselves far
more frequently in contact with congressmen than with
senators.

It is not easy to convey the strange, subtle, and constantly
shifting relationships that develop between the representatives
of education interests and the world of congressional power and
influence. As in most human relations, there are felicities as well
as tensions in the chemistry of personalities. The arrogance of
power is not unknown on Capitol Hill; brashness and stupidity
are not unknown among lobbyists. Some educators indulge in
intellectual hubris and in academic narcissism that drive political
types up the wall. Some legislators and a few staff members
convey to academic petitioners a sense that a simple request for
help is an act of lèse majesté. But there is an in-group of a dozen
or so legislative types on the one hand and an equal number of
education representatives on the other who are in the game together. They may get miffed at one another on occasion and they
do not always see eye to eye; but they are basically dependent
on one another. This mutual dependence takes a number of
forms, but in essence the trade is one of expertise and service
from the education side for sympathetic consideration by the
political side. If expertise turns out to be wanting, sympathetic
consideration dwindles. On the other hand, if relevant expertise
is patent and sustained, the education spokesman finds himself
on the fringes of legislative mark-up sessions—making history
anonymously along with a thirty-two-year-old staff expert, one
or two executive branch specialists, and a couple of preoccupied
legislators.

Association services to legislators and their staffs vary substantially. At one extreme, they involve a substantial exercise of political power. In 1972, Senator Claiborne Pell, chairman of the Education Subcommittee of the Senate Committee on Labor and Public Welfare, found himself in the toughest political campaign of his life. All signs pointed to the election of his competitor, John Chaffee, then governor of Rhode Island. AFL/CIO, NEA, and AFT, through appropriate political arms, made campaign contributions of money or direct services that probably saved him. As a result, although Senator Pell would not now automatically press for what these friends request legislatively (for one thing they do not always see eye to eye among themselves), he and his staff have additional good reasons for listening to them with sympathetic respect. Since reelection is a major goal of most congressmen and senators, help in this crucial arena of political combat is recognized by education associations as a particularly important means of establishing, at the very least, sympathetic access. It is for this reason, for example, that in the 1972 campaign, NEA, which prides itself on being the largest professional association in the world, found ways of using both money and "person power" in 184 congressional races. "The candidates they supported won in 128 of 165 House contests and in 13 of 19 Senate races."[13] As we shall note in the final chapter, 1974 campaign activities were even greater. If NEA and AFT should succeed in an effective merger, and if NEA's political alliance with the state, county, and municipal workers union is sustained, the direct political influence of education on congressional fortunes—and perhaps on Presidential fortunes—may be considerably enhanced in the future. NEA plans a political war chest of millions of dollars for the 1976 campaign.

Education associations can give congressmen and senators a number of other political assists. One simple device is providing

13. *NEA NOW*, Nov. 13, 1972.

an important local, state, regional, or national forum for a speech. Legislators need publicity. It is an essential aspect of developing and sustaining political support. A speech before a conference of educators has a triple political benefit: it carries a message directly to an important group of citizens; it links the legislator with a large number of influential citizens; and it commands the attention of the media. To those in associations who are putting a program together for an annual convention, the availability of an influential and titled speaker is often a godsend. Everyone benefits—everyone, that is, if the speech is worth hearing and is well delivered.

Friendly mention of a legislator in a newsletter or in a voting tally is often helpful. Other services of associations for members of Congress include writing speeches, drafting bills, preparing news releases, gathering witnesses to testify before a subcommittee, doing "head counts" before a floor vote, helping to draft committee reports, organizing pressures on a key but recalcitrant committee member, lining up other associations for or against a particular bill, and compiling and analyzing data needed in law making and in program review. So intimate are the relationships on many of these activities that it is hard to know where public and private influence and activities begin and leave off.

All these close working relationships are a far cry from what is normally exposed to public view: the formal testimony or submitted statements of associations provided to congressional committees at their request. To the sophisticated lobbyists, formal hearings are almost totally meretricious. They rarely change congressional minds. In any case, most testimony can be predicted by an astute staff member with considerable accuracy. Furthermore, at many formal hearings, a lone legislator with a couple of staff members gives whatever continuity there is to the issue at hand. Frequently, the main functions of formal testimony and prepared statements are to convince grass-roots clientele that an association is on its toes and to assure friendly staff members and congressmen that the associations stand ready to assist them in the formalities of carrying out the rituals of democracy. Occasionally, formal presentations to committees receive general press coverage. More frequently, they provide copy for the house organs of the associations involved.

These paragraphs of general description hide, of course, as much as they reveal, for the congressional world is complex. It swirls with eddies of controversy that muddy virtually all associational contacts. Perhaps thirty to forty congressional subcommittees are involved in important aspects of education legislation. What pleases one subcommittee or individual legislator may alienate another. An association's access to one center of power may be countered by hostility elsewhere. Personality, as well as ideological, clashes among members of the House Education and Labor Committee and between Senate and House conferees frustrated key spokesmen for higher education's interests during and following the conference committee's struggle over the Education Amendments of 1972. Some of the pressure tactics used by the Committee for the Full Funding of Education Programs in recent years (to increase appropriations for education beyond the amounts requested by the President) have delighted some members of Congress but infuriated others.

All of these controversies are compounded when the administration is of one party and the two houses of Congress are controlled by the other party. To use an analogy from sailing, when pro-education Presidential, bureaucratic, and House and Senate politics all blow in the same direction, education associations find themselves "running free." When these various centers of force are variable and gusty, interest group seamanship is put to the test. All one can say is that clear and steady political winds have been rare in recent decades. Even partisan affiliation is no clear indication of educational stance. Many Republican congressmen and senators have sided with their Democratic colleagues on key education issues.

The Cultivation of the Grass Roots

Partly because of the antilobbying provisions of Section 501 (c)(3), partly because of obvious political reality, many education associations try to influence congressional behavior less by direct contact than by a careful cultivation of grass-roots pressures. Few conglomerates of interest have more effective grass-roots networks—at least potentially—than education. Education is incomparably the largest and most ubiquitous social enterprise in the nation. Schools, principals, teachers, school board members, students, colleges, interested parents, faculty members, and trustees are found in every state and in every important center of population.

In spite of public disenchantments with parts of the education system, educators are generally esteemed members of communities. School boards and boards of trustees often include some of the most influential citizens in an area. Teacher power, particularly, has increased dramatically across the country in recent years.[14] Under NEA and AFT leadership, teachers are increasingly involved in campaign financing and election activities.

The most sophisticated education organizations, by themselves and also with other groups, develop networks of grass-roots influence that can be exploited on a particular issue with considerable dispatch. Normally, these networks are by states or regions; and in some cases they are organized nationally by subject matter, by types of institutions, or through a national "governmental relations committee" that is geographically balanced. When an issue arises on Capitol Hill, the affected association will try to identify the important legislative actors, and will then ask their local or area contacts to identify persons influential at the grass roots who are associated with or friendly to education in the states or congressional districts of those mem-

14. Walter Mossberg, "Teacher Power," *Wall Street Journal*, Aug. 21, 1974.

bers of Congress. Sometimes such influential constituents come to Washington for direct communications or to present testimony. Sometimes they telephone or telegraph their opinion. Sometimes they write a letter, either to the congressman or to the local paper. Legislators tend to follow local newspapers with microscopic care.

The Washington-based associations help to keep state and local "government relations" workers or "government liaison" workers informed of substantive and tactical developments through newsletters and special reports. For example, the American Personnel and Guidance Association put out "Legislative Fliers" for the benefit of the "Legislative Chairman" of its state branches "offering suggestions on the most effective means to inform Congress of the needs of youth and of the profession."[15] The National University Extension Association has "regions" across the country, each region with a network of respondents who can develop grass-roots contacts with specific senators and representatives on any occasion. On April 2, 1971, for example, NUEA sent out a duplicated "Governmental Relations Action Bulletin" to its regional and institutional network. One section especially is typical of legislative action summaries issued by the most active education associations in Washington.

» Our situation is this: If the additional funds for title I are included in the substitute bill, we will alert the Governmental Relations Committee network. Committee members will have to take immediate action in their respective states to get as many institutions, state agency people and other individuals who participate in, or are interested in title I programs to contact their Congressmen (not their Senators at this time) *by wire or phone call* "to support the substitute bill for the Office of Education Appropriation." The vote will take place

15. APGA *Highlights, 1952–1972.*

on Wednesday, April 7, so that the calls must be made on the 5th or 6th if they are to be meaningful.

The Influential Few

The activities described in this chapter are characteristic of only a few education associations. The great majority are politically weak or, at most, gain marginal influence over events by providing general information and opinion through newsletters and journals to their clienteles.

Even the active few have a mixed record. Few of the few have a policy analysis capability, rhetorical resources, and an information delivery system that enable them to be powerful participants in educational policy making on the Hill or in the executive branch. But at their best, the best of the few can and do make a difference, and by the means described above.

CHAPTER FIVE

The Unfinished Agenda

INITIALLY, this monograph was planned to include two additional chapters. One was to describe the relationship of education associations to their clienteles; the second was to explore the relationships among education associations. However, the research was interrupted in 1973, and subsequent priorities have precluded my giving adequate attention to these important topics. Had opportunity permitted, I would have fleshed out some of the following skeletal propositions:

◊ Many national education associations have intermediate clienteles, "intermediate clienteles" defined to include the officers of state and local affiliates of national organizations. Relating effectively and simultaneously to sensitive intermediate clienteles as well as to ultimate clienteles (individual institutions, groups, and persons) involves both art and luck. Repair of disjunctures can be time consuming and enervating.

◊ Many an education association includes members whose interests and values diverge widely. The harmonizing of diverse interests can often be troublesome to the point of immobilizing efforts on key issues of public policy.

◊ Clienteles vary substantially in their insistence on formal clearance procedures on policy issues. Those associations that must wait for their membership's formal voice in plenary session, and whose executive staffs are thereby denied the right and capacity to react to policy issues as they arise, are not among the powerful.

◊ Associations that work together nationally with relative ease and effectiveness sometimes have clientele groups that are at each other's throats in the field.

◊ Education associations work together on many national issues, break away at other times to find new and temporary partners, and come together again with their original friends. Over time, they react more favorably to a relationship of easy, reciprocal catalysis than they do to coordination by some one group's assumed preeminence.

◊ In the interaction of associations, leadership tends to be a function of knowledge and contacts. Increasingly "knowledge" involves high-powered policy analysis capabilities; "contacts" include effective activity in grass-roots communications and politics.

◊ Factors of personality and accidents of timing make the role of interest groups in policy making less predictable than policy scientists might hope.

This mixture of fairly obvious propositions and banal "theorettes" is offered at this point to help complete the stage furniture needed for the final act of this monograph.

What is the unfinished agenda for education interest groups at the national level? Well-meaning critics of education's Washington representation have written extensive reports and less extensive essays on this theme for a number of years. Some of these have been published; many have been private or limited-circulation reports; some have been speeches or conference summaries.[1] As might be expected, not all critics agree.

1. See particularly: George W. McGurn, "New Patterns in Government-Higher Education Relationships," mimeographed (Paper presented at the 1974 National Conference on Public Administration, April 1974); Daniel P.

Education groups, or significant levels thereof, have been told by some to "get it all together" and to speak as one voice. For years this was the warning and the advice of the late Senator Wayne Morse of Oregon. When, in 1972, the higher education associations *did* get together on "institutional aid," they were then told by senators and congressmen that they had got together on the wrong issue. Furthermore, sophisticated legislators and their staffs and executive branch officials know full well that there are legitimate differences of interest among various segments of the education community. To those in government who know these differences are logical, it is frustrating and maddening to have a laundered policy presentation that seems to bleach out all diversity of hue in the rich tapestry of interest-group priorities.

There is a related point. At times there are plaintive calls from legislative or executive staffs for interest-group help in making hard allocative choices among contending claimants within a limited overall budget. Within loose limits of "caucus" bargaining, such help can occasionally be proferred. But loose coalitions do not stay together happily or for long if the stronger members criticize or override the weaker ones before official eyes and ears.

Moynihan, "The Politics of Higher Education," *Daedalus*, Winter 1975, pp. 128–247; Lewis N. Pino, *Nothing but Praise: Thoughts on the Ties between Higher Education and the Federal Government* (Lincoln: Nebraska Curriculum Development Center, 1972); Louis W. Bender and Howard L. Simmons, *One Dupont Circle: National Influence Center for Higher Education?* (Tallahassee: Florida State University, Division of Education Management Systems, November 1973); Edith K. Mosher, "The Politics of Higher Education during the Nixon Administration," mimeographed (Address at the 1973 meeting of the American Educational Research Association, New Orleans, La., Feb. 28, 1973); John C. Honey and John C. Crowley, "The Future of the American Council on Education: A Report on Its Governmental and Related Activities," mimeographed (September 1972); Roger W. Heyns, "The National Educational Establishment," *Educational Record*, Spring 1973, pp. 93–99.

At least some overburdened officials, legislators, and staffs wish there might be an external, objective think-tank to analyze all the conflicting claims and the kaleidescopic data of competing educational interests and give decision-makers a balanced and objective report on what in fact *is* in the public interest. But in education, as in other sectors of the society, there are no omniscient, wholly impartial experts. There are intelligent people with a conscience in the handling of evidence, both within interest groups and outside them. On the outside, the Brookings Institution, for example, has an enviable reputation for analytic sophistication and scholarly care in handling economic and social data. But to pretend that Brookings scholars are uncommitted to sets of particular social values is to defame them. Similarly, Clark Kerr's Carnegie Council on Policy Studies in Higher Education, other educational policy research centers, various regional education laboratories and university-based research and development centers, and individual researchers and commentators—all these include some first-rate scholars, statisticians, and analysts. But so do the AFL/CIO, NEA, the National Industrial Conference Board, and ACE.

The real safety for society will lie, not in creating a new think-tank for education, but in maintaining a diversity of partially overlapping centers and scholarly endeavors around the country—a diversity sufficient to ensure high-quality peer review of what any one center or person produces. Ultimately, interest groups cannot substitute their internal bargaining for the tough political allocations that can be made only by politically accountable decision-makers.

If education interest groups cannot expect to speak with one voice, can they improve their analytic capacity and can they work together more effectively in the cause of broad and common educational concerns? The answer seems clearly to be yes. The debacle for higher education associations in the struggle over the Education Amendments of 1972, as noted earlier, was in part not of their own making. Personality and power contests on Capitol Hill caught higher education in a vicious mangle. But higher education did not have a policy research and data system adequate to meet the kinds of questions put by both friends and enemies on the Hill. The American Council on Education has attempted since then to improve its capacity in this area by creating a Policy Analysis Service and a Division of Educational Statistics. Other higher education associations have pioneered in selected fields: for example, the American Association of State Colleges and Universities and the Education Commission of the States, in the field of state policy developments; the Association of American Colleges, in the fields of women's rights and collective bargaining; the American Association for Higher Education, in educational innovation. NEA has created a separate nonprofit research staff: the National Foundation for the Improvement of Education. Together with NEA's own policy research staff, NFIE informs and enlightens the education decision processes of the nation. All of these are now or are becoming nationally recognized information resource centers. In addition, many education associations act as brokers between research sponsors and research agents—facilitating the contracting out of studies that are of interest to the associations and to their clienteles.

In short, education's information and analytic services are far better than they once were. There are daily prods from policy-planning and accountability staffs at the federal and state levels to induce education associations to improve these capabilities even further. The report of the National Commission on the Financing of Postsecondary Education in 1973 was a healthy review of the state of the art, and provided a series of seminal models for future data gathering and analyses.[2] The Budget and Impoundment Control Act of 1974 will impose new de-

2. *Financing Postsecondary Education in the United States* (Washington: Government Printing Office, 1973).

mands on all of the major education associations. Not only will better data and analyses be needed to support favored programs, but also education interest groups will have to develop compelling justifications for education's adequate share of the federal budget vis-à-vis other, competing social needs. This latter exercise will call for new ranges of analytic skills going beyond, but including, education as a major policy area.

Unfortunately, the educational statistical services of the federal government—the data font for much of the analytic work done by the education associations—have been woefully underfinanced and inadequate. In 1974, the National Center for Education Statistics was moved from the U.S. Office of Education to the Office of the Assistant Secretary for Education of the Department of Health, Education, and Welfare. The organizational shift will be meaningless unless a prestigious and able staff and adequate funding are secured. The nation spends five times as much on health statistics as it does on education statistics. The capacity of the education associations to improve their data compilation and analyses will depend largely on the willingness of education interest groups and, especially, of Congress to support a comprehensive federal education data enterprise.

On "getting together," improvements have also been made. In recent years, an inner corps of personal friendships and common interests have made it possible for NEA, AFT, NSBA, CCSSO, and key staffs of the AFL/CIO to work together on legislative strategies across a wide range of issues. The Big Six (NAESP, NASSP, AASA, NASBE, CCSSO, NSBA) find periodic opportunities to review policy agenda and to take common stands on issues affecting precollegiate education as a whole. At the higher education level, the American Council on Education continues to be a catalyst and broker among the several major associations of colleges and universities. It is attempting to develop more effective ways of mobilizing and orchestrating the policy research and governmental relations staffs in the National Center for Higher Education and beyond.

Again, however, far more needs to be done. Yet four inter-related dangers could preclude effective representation for education in Washington in the critical years ahead. First is the danger that internecine warfare between faculty unions and educational management (school boards, superintendents, boards of regents, chief state school officers, college and university boards and executives) could become so bitter regionally and locally as to imperil unity on major issues of national support for education. Washington-based education associations and organizations must attempt to contain and to isolate the bitterness of local and intrainstitutional conflicts so that a reasonably united front can be presented to the federal government on major issues of educational policy.

Second is the danger of destructive competition among teachers unions. NEA, AFT, and, at the higher education level, AAUP are engaged in collective-bargaining-agent battles across the nation. This internecine war, even when transcended at the national level on specific issues, causes resources to be diverted away from more basic policy issues. As the contests become more vigorous, they can easily hobble healthy cooperative relationships in the Washington arena. Previous note has been made of the fact that NEA's political alliance with the American Federation of State, County and Municipal Employees adds high drama to an already complex story of education interest group competition.

Third is the danger of associational fragmentation and jealousy. Higher education associations, for example, are caught between the need for more effective collaboration and the need for associational identity and focus. As noted at the start of chapter 3, education's representatives, in addition to wanting protection from harm and wanting favorable rules and resources for their constituencies, want "respectability and recognition," for themselves. Education association work in Washington is not uniformly recognized as high-prestige activity. When I accepted the vice-presidency of the American Council on Education, a top educator in the government commented, "My God! Do you *really* want to be a *lobbyist*?" The acid skepticism dripped. Many executive directors and governmental relations officers of the education organizations have held prestigious positions. Some, seemingly now whipsawed by clientele pressures and demands for deference by appointed and elected officials and their staffs, find parts of their lives marginally demeaning. In moments of resiliency, they know that being on the frontiers of advocacy for the support and improvement of educational services and opportunities is a high privilege. But when advocacy involves extensive accommodation to the interests of other education associations and groups, even an ebullient sense of identity and discrete function can be eroded. "The coalition did it" is not the same psychically as "we did it"; and "we did it" is not the same psychically as "I did it"—especially when several "coalition" activities may call into question the need for separate "we" and "I" activities. The very establishment of a Washington office (and more are emerging monthly) creates ipso facto a need for self-justification and makes interassociational cooperation tentative and strained.

There must be room in the "getting-together" process for what Kahlil Gibran called "spaces in our togetherness." But representatives must also find increased ego satisfaction in effective cooperation. Education associations must negotiate these delicate relationships with sensitivity and mutual understanding.

Finally, there is the danger of political innocence on the one side and in contraproductive political activism on the other. In recent years, NEA has made a basic choice to "go political." It was deeply involved in the political process in 1974, even more so than in 1972. In 1974, "NEA's Political Action Committee said it endorsed 310 Federal office seekers in 48 states, including

165 who received financial contributions amounting to $225,000. In addition, . . . state and local association political action groups contributed $2.5 million to Federal, state and local races. . . . Teacher-supported candidates won in 229 of 282 House contests and were successful in 21 of 28 Senate races."[3] This, of course, is too simple. Multiple causes of victory were at work in most cases. But no one should underestimate the importance of the NEA activity for the future of federal educational policies. Even larger political activities are being planned for the Presidential election of 1976. Teacher power is increasing across the land. As long as the major teacher organizations concentrate on the quality of education and the needs of students as well as on teacher benefits, and as long as friends in all parties are supported, political activity has a good chance of carrying with it substantial public support. But if teacher politics appears to be narrowly partisan and a self-serving raid on the public treasury, no amount of organized political activity will produce lasting benefits for the educational sector broadly conceived. What is true of teachers in this regard is true of all segments of education.

Most education associations, of course, have neither the membership nor the budget to indulge in electoral strategies and tactics. They have to cultivate political friends in other ways: through information, through rhetoric, through services, through prudent stimulation of grass-roots responses to political dangers and opportunities.

"Political friends" means something beyond elected politicians. Education needs the political support of other major interests in the society: business, labor, agriculture, veterans, other professions. Educational institutions, associations, and organizations must work at all levels of society—local, state, and national—to develop the understanding and to win the confidence of persons

3. *Higher Education and National Affairs*, Nov. 15, 1974, p. 4.

influential in other fields of endeavor—persons whose political significance is manifest in the substantive and procedural deliberations of the polity. Schools, colleges, and universities need the understanding and support of chambers of commerce, of manufacturers associations, of farm groups, of labor unions, of bar associations, of veterans organizations. Most of these groups start out with a favorable view of the importance of education. But educators far too often take such groups for granted or treat them with more than a tinge of disdain. Increased and improved contact with the pluralistic centers of real political strength in our democracy is a long, unfinished agenda for most educational institutions, associations, and organizations.

Equally, attention must be spent on improving education's contacts within the executive branch of the federal government. This has been touched on earlier. Suffice it to say that inhospitalities and frustrations during the Nixon years led far too many education interest groups to ignore the appropriate cultivation of bureaucrats and political executives. Under President Ford, the personal climate is warmer although the policy climate remains cool. In brief, the executive branch is a mighty force in policy formulation. Education interest groups neglect its various facets at considerable long-range peril.

A related matter is attention to the possibilities of the media in developing public understanding and support. Controversy over education, like all other controversy, is newsworthy (sometimes education gets more media attention than it wants). Except for the area of sports coverage, educational institutions and their associations tend to pay far too little attention to human-interest materials that tell a positive story of education's essentiality to personal enrichment and to societal problem solving. In the nation's capital, the *Washington Post* and the *New York Times* are especially important instruments of communication to national leaders, although weekly, monthly, and quarterly journals and radio and TV are all part of the network of opportunity for telling education's story. This goes far beyond traditional public relations. Every day, things happen in the schools and colleges of our nation that deserve public attention: quiet successes in racial integration, aesthetic creations of merit, new teaching and learning technologies, scientific inventions and medical advances, curricular changes introduced to deal with the environment or with international interdependence. Too often these stories are not told at all, or are communicated in arcane and recondite journals where they are inaccessible to legislators, officials, and the public at large. The society's sense of the importance of the educational enterprise cannot be left to chance or to trade journals. Education associations must work far more assiduously than they have in the past in telling education's story to those media that have the greatest impact on both the public at large and its political leaders.

The associations must also work far harder than they have to date at the problem of newsletters, bulletins, action guides, and fact sheets that emanate from education's Washington offices, particularly those in the field of higher education. The duplication of news and analysis represented in association publications and in a limited number of commercial outlets sometimes wastes both money and time. Often the level of factual detail is too ponderous to be useful to the reader; political analyses are frequently lacking in political action guidelines.

Finally, higher education associations must do far more than they have to tap the brains they represent. In-house policy and governmental relations staffs are not enough. Scores of higher education institutions spread around the country have in-house institutional research staffs, faculty, and graduate students capable of preparing data and analyses designed to illuminate and to help solve educational policy problems. These talents have not been adequately identified and mobilized.

All of the above, of course, is gimmickry unless educational institutions are able to maintain and improve the basic services for which they exist. Public and political support is ultimately a function of performance that is valued. No amount of sophisticated association activity can compensate for loss of public confidence in the ongoing activities of the enterprise. If educational institutions and programs are peopled by time-servers mired in bureaucratic practices, unable to assist the slow and excite the talented, contemptuous of standards of excellence, preoccupied with custodial tranquility, self-serving rather than client-oriented in their mission, no amount of interest-group and association activity will produce public support.

Ultimately, the success of education's representation depends upon the quality of educational services that are rendered to the people of the United States.

Index of Organizations

The various associations and organizations listed in this index are meant to serve as examples. The omission of any given organization should not be construed as indicating a judgment about its value or importance.

AMERICAN COUNCIL ON EDUCATION

Roger W. Heyns, *President*

The American Council on Education, founded in 1918 and composed of institutions of higher education and national and regional education associations, is the nation's major coordinating body for postsecondary education. Through voluntary and cooperative action, the Council provides comprehensive leadership for improving educational standards, policies, and procedures.